Critical Guides to French Texts

51 Bernardin de Saint-Pierre: Paul et Virginie

Critical Guides to French Texts

EDITED BY ROGER LITTLE, WOLFGANG VAN EMDEN, DAVID WILLIAMS

BERNARDIN DE SAINT-PIERRE

Paul et Virginie

Philip Robinson

Lecturer in French,
University of Kent, Canterbury

Grant & Cutler Ltd
1986

© Grant & Cutler Ltd
1986
ISBN 0 7293 0228 8

I.S.B.N. 84-599-1112-8

DEPÓSITO LEGAL: V. 2.032 - 1985

Printed in Spain by
Artes Gráficas Soler, S.A., Valencia
for
GRANT & CUTLER LTD
11 BUCKINGHAM STREET, LONDON W.C.2

Contents

For my mother

Prefatory Note

I express my warm thanks to my colleague Vivienne Mylne for reading this study in typescript and for her helpful comments and suggestions. I also thank Mr Ian G. Smith of Canterbury, formerly resident in Mauritius, for the loan of maps and books on the island which it would have been time-consuming to find elsewhere. My indebtedness to previous scholars, and in particular to the late Jean Fabre, is considerable. Without allowing the references to become too obtrusive, I have preferred to indicate such debts in the text, where they may be followed up in context.

References to the text of *Paul et Virginie* are to the edition presented by Robert Mauzi (Paris, Garnier-Flammarion, 1966). This edition provides a chronological outline of the life of Bernardin de Saint-Pierre (pp.5-10).

References to works listed in the Select Bibliography give the number of the work in italics, the number of the individual volume, if appropriate, in Roman numerals, followed by the page numbers, thus: *4*, III, pp.137-38.

Introduction

Jacques-Henri-Bernardin de Saint-Pierre's *Paul et Virginie* (1788) is one of the most neglected of that limited number of novels which form the French eighteenth-century canon. When it is read nowadays it is also fairly commonly misunderstood. The neglect and the misunderstanding, which are connected, have to do with the radical differences of taste, philosophy and social attitudes between the late eighteenth and the late twentieth centuries. The modern reader, encouraged by current orthodoxy to consider himself creative and to treat his immediate reading experience as legitimate and authoritative, may be forgiven (if he is not a critic) for seeing the novel as merely a period piece, quite as dated as a periwig or frilly cuffs.

Compared with most novels which enjoy the status of being taught as school or university texts, the story of *Paul et Virginie* is extremely simple. A boy and a girl are brought up together by their mothers in a secluded valley of a tropical island in the Indian Ocean, as if they were brother and sister. At puberty the girl is sent away, on the insistence of a rich but cruel maiden great-aunt, to France, where she is to receive a proper education for polite society and ultimately the great-aunt's fortune. However, because she finally refuses the idea of marriage with anyone but the boy with whom she has been brought up, she is after a few years rejected by this same great-aunt and sent back, during the cyclone season, to the island of her birth. Her ship is within one day of arriving when it is trapped and destroyed by a storm on the north-eastern coast of the island, and she is drowned. Overcome by grief, the two mothers, the boy, one male slave, one female slave, and a dog, all follow her within a matter of months into the grave. The cruel great-aunt outlives them all, but only for a time and in a torment of bitterness, remorse and humiliation, since avaricious relatives, avid for her inheritance, finally have her locked up as a lunatic.

Presented in this way, in cold blood, the story may raise a smile. Yet the sad and simple tale of young dreams thwarted was, and remains, for all the complex and often extremely beautiful literary fabric which Bernardin weaves around it, the book's principal appeal. Reading it we are to enjoy having a good cry. It is mistaken to try to play this fact down: it must be constantly borne in mind when other aspects of the text are elaborated upon. Those other aspects indeed nearly all serve to heighten in some way or other this central emotional appeal. The story's simplicity, moreover, should not lead us to prejudge anything about its literary merit. Many of the great works of world literature could be similarly reduced to a simple outline. Indeed, as a preliminary exercise, it can be instructive, and sometimes amusing, to do so. Whatever literary merit is, simplicity of story-line makes little difference to it. In *Paul et Virginie* the simplicity and the basic emotional appeal are bare facts with which we have to reckon.

There is also a problem, we shall see, in describing the work as a novel. What the word 'novel' means to us is different from what its equivalent, *'roman'*, meant to the generation of Bernardin. This would not matter if it did not influence our ideas about whether *Paul et Virginie* is a good 'novel'. Of course, as with food, we may insist that we know what we like. This often means that we like what is familiar and are reluctant to try anything different. So we are with foreign food, and so we are, not infrequently, with the literature of the past; for the past, as the dictum says, is 'another country'. What help is there for the person who demands of its inhabitants: 'Why don't they all speak English?'? A certain wonderment and surprised curiosity are essential if we are to communicate with this 'other country'. If we pay too much attention to its rebarbative differences, they will become like the fly in the ointment: a minute and insignificant speck, but one which takes away all our appreciation.

The fly in the ointment is only too easy to dwell upon with Bernardin's tale: excessive sentimentality, paucity of incident, prudish attitudes to sex, condescension towards women, apparent acquiescence with regard to slavery. These faults are less serious than they seem, and the last one, at least, is illusory.

A dash of historical imagination is essential if we are to get the most out of the book, and that is why I begin with the exotic setting. As an aid to imagination, I include the following map.

1. The Exotic Setting

Paul et Virginie is normally credited with introducing exoticism into French literature. This is true, however, only if we understand it in a precise way. Things foreign can have mystery and charm, and the point was exploited in literature well before Bernardin de Saint-Pierre. There are examples from the ancient world and from the medieval romances, and in the more recent past there were the translation into French of the *Arabian Nights* (1711), Montesquieu's *Lettres persanes*, Prévost's *Manon Lescaut* (the last section of which transports us to America with the heroine), Voltaire's *Orphelin de la Chine* and Diderot's *Supplément au voyage de Bougainville*. One may of course add to this list, but in each case the exotic setting is either fantastic and unreal, or purely imagined (Prévost's America), or largely constructed from documentary sources (Montesquieu's Persia and Diderot's Tahiti).

Bernardin is original in taking the setting for his fiction from his own personal observations during a stay on Mauritius (then the Ile de France) between 1768 and 1770, and in not embellishing it with fanciful and extraordinary detail. Memory may add lustre to his scenes, as compared, say, to his *Voyage à l'Ile de France (3)*, but his eyes have beh ld what his pen describes. His military posting to the Indian Ocean as 'Capitaine d'infanterie, Ingénieur du Roi à l'Ile de France' was the last great adventure of an adventurous and vagabond youth. And it was not really as grand as it sounds. Despite the title of his commission, he was actually bound for one of the French forts on Madagascar, but, having quarrelled with his commander-in-chief on board ship, he was, before they arrived, put ashore on Mauritius on 14 July 1768. This was socially awkward for him, not only because he had no practical place in the French military establishment of the island, but also because he had no family background to sustain him.

He was the son of a respectable government official in Le Havre and, despite his constant efforts to prove the contrary, had no noble ancestry. He was given a reasonably good formal education, culminating in a spell of scientific training at the Ecole des Ponts et Chaussées in Paris. He suffered with others as the government, owing to the Seven Years' War (1756-63), sent the pupils home in 1758 before they had gained their diplomas. His ambitions had thus been given a military orientation but with no qualifications to back them up. He was destined to be a misfit and a wanderer for the best part of fifteen years. That part of his life (1758-71) is full of adventure, amorous and otherwise, as he enjoys a succession of favours and short-lived posts with different European governments, first in Europe itself (Malta, Holland, Prussia, Russia, Finland and Poland) and finally in Mauritius.

The essential point about this vagabond life is that Bernardin kept his eyes open, not only on the human scene, but also on the landscapes, no small achievement when one considers the sheer physical punishment of travelling, by land or sea, at this period. Long sea voyages in particular (it took more than four months to reach Mauritius) involved cramped conditions, a high risk of diseases such as scurvy, and considerable danger. His copious correspondence is punctuated with descriptions which are really essays in literary landscape. Many of his letters already show the capacities for accurate observation and for powerful graphic evocation which are characteristic of the later, published, works. His first significant piece of writing, the *Voyage à l'Ile de France* (1773), tells in letter form the story of his two sea voyages and has a detailed description of the flora, fauna and human *mores* of the French colony. Bernardin hoped, with the help of this text, to win the favour of the French government. It was a vain hope, precisely because his objective observations differed so markedly from the exaggeration and embroidery of most previous 'extraordinary voyages'. He also allowed it to be seen that his experience of the place was not a wholly pleasant one. Above all, he presented an unflattering picture of the island's whites and an attack on black slavery. The *Voyage* contains more detail of the natural history of the island than does *Paul et*

Virginie, and has considerable merit and importance as a piece of travel writing and as an anti-slavery tract.

   Bernardin saw much of the local colour of the island, whether in his military capacity as, in his phrase, a building site foreman, or on his botanising trips with the Intendant, M. Poivre, or on the social round in amorous pursuit (unsuccessfully) of the Intendant's wife. But perhaps even more importantly for his future novel *Paul et Virginie*, he encountered the folk-lore of the island, and in particular the story of a famous shipwreck, a generation previously, on 17 August 1744. This catastrophe, one of the more noteworthy among many, had really happened, with considerable loss of life, to the *Saint-Géran*, a relatively large vessel with a carrying capacity of 600 *tonneaux* (see *20*, pp.75-76). Stories were due to the nine survivors (since nobody actually witnessed the disaster from the shore) and to the spreading of information from government reports drafted within weeks of the event. The historical documents have been examined and published (see *17*), and the comparison of these with the novel suggests that Bernardin did not work from written sources in constructing his tale but from his memory of what he heard while on the island. The literary imagination, whether reflected by folk-lore or by the pen of a sophisticated European, tends to transfigure such events. One nice example, and an important one for *Paul et Virginie*, is the motif of refusing to undress and to save oneself thereby from the waves. In the story this becomes the famous scene of the doomed Virginie looking skyward on the deck of the sinking ship and refusing the pleas of the naked sailor to join him in like condition in a swim for the shore (p.159). In the official accounts it is the captain who refuses to disrobe!

   We simply have no way of knowing in what form Bernardin heard the circulating stories of the famous wreck. It is worth-while to examine the historical documents, if only to realise the extent to which Bernardin's creative imagination has changed them in his fictional account. The documented history is not the source of his story but one of the chosen constraints of its narrative convention. For example, he hesitated a long time before finally placing the event in its correct historical year (though still not on its correct historical date): he knew that the island as described in his novel is more developed economically, with plantations, a vigorous trade with India, and a social circle of fine ladies, than the historical Ile de France just beginning to feel the effects of La Bourdonnais's policies in 1738-39. In the end he opts for the correct year of the shipwreck, which is one of the few well-known facts about it.

Bernardin probably began while he was still on the island to sketch ideas for what was to become *Paul et Virginie*. He worked on it actively from his return to France (June 1771) and well before publication of the *Voyage* (1773). Indeed, when he planned to revise the *Voyage* because of its lack of success by making it far more of a personal chronicle, he considered including with it the earliest complete draft of his tale, which still exists in manuscript, called *Histoire de Mlle Virginie de la Tour*. This draft was complete by 1777 or shortly after, but the proposed revision of the *Voyage* came to nothing, so, despite being complete and publishable, the story remained a manuscript.

Here I must digress to say that the years 1771-84 are difficult ones for Bernardin. He is back in France, that is, principally in Paris, and the vagabond life is over. He has plenty of experience but no material success to show for it. He keeps going with loans from his many friends, and his charm, especially with women, contributes to his survival. Despite a deep melancholy in this period, he reacts positively and works hard, not only, in the 1770s, on the draft of his tale, but also on the *Etudes de la nature* (1784). This work, in three volumes comprising twelve books, is a spirited defence of the idea of a personal Providence, a critique of the kind of science which sets itself apart from morality and leads men towards atheism, and an apology for an extreme form of the Socratic attitude, the conviction that enquiries which do not contribute directly to a knowledge of Man and of God are to be resisted. All these standpoints resemble those of Jean-Jacques Rousseau closely, but with important differences. Rousseau believes in a general Providence and not an individual and personal one, and he has a much sharper sense than Bernardin of the difference between the disciplines of natural philosophy (or science) and moral philosophy. At any rate, to anybody schooled in the basic ideas of normal science in our own day, the *Etudes* are full of crazy notions, including denials of magnetism and electricity and the rejection of lunar gravitational effects on the tides. This 'system' is nevertheless underpinned with many quite superb passages, describing various beauties of Nature, which have no antecedents in French literature. Indeed the term *Etudes* is to be understood more in the artistic sense of 'sketches' than in its scientific meaning.

The *Etudes*, to which we shall return briefly in a later chapter, made Bernardin's name in more senses than one. Baptised Jacques-Bernardin-Henri de Saint-Pierre in 1737, he tells us in the *Préambule* to *Paul et Virginie* (p.45) that the title page of the *Etudes* accidentally changed this to Jacques-Henri-Bernardin. Very quickly readers interpreted this final forename as a family name, with the erroneous inference that 'de Saint-Pierre' marked the family territory or estate. He was happy to let this impression continue, since, like many other ambitious young men with no background to speak of, he had, since his very first wanderings, styled himself 'chevalier de Saint-Pierre', implying that he was the impoverished younger son of a noble family. 'Bernardin' we still call him.

Paul et Virginie, an extensive revision of the manuscript *Histoire de Mlle Virginie de la Tour* (see *2*), was eventually published in 1788 as part of a new, fourth, volume of the *Etudes de la nature*. The significance of the connection should not be exaggerated, but it is real. Bernardin already showed his concern, in the abortive project to publish the *Histoire* with a revised version of the *Voyage*, to present his tale as part of an evocation of the real life and local colour of the Indian Ocean. Now the emphasis is slightly different: the story is offered as a kind of illustration of the theses of the *Etudes*. The *Avant-propos* of 1788 declares that it has a similar moral aim: 'Je me suis proposé d'y mettre en évidence plusieurs grandes vérités, entre autres celle-ci: que notre bonheur consiste à vivre suivant la nature et la vertu' (p.177). Undoubtedly, Bernardin has another, more down-to-earth, motive for launching the story in this way: he hopes that the proven success of the *Etudes* (now in its third edition) will be a 'vehicle' for the new material. It is nevertheless true that his quaint theories are the ideological driving force without which we should not possess his remarkable and original descriptions of natural beauties. These are important to him precisely because, like Rousseau before him, he subscribes to the 'pathetic fallacy', the belief that visible and tangible Nature corresponds intimately with the human mind and spirit. Meticulous observation and annotation are a kind of Nature-worship.

Roughly one fifth of the story is taken up with description of scenery, that is if we include the account of the 'landscaping' of the high valley settlement, and exclude the odd short lines which appear as a part of other sections, such as the Rivière Noire adventure. Judging purely by the space they occupy, therefore, these descriptions are important in more than one way. Looked at in isolation, their first noticeable quality is their precision and clarity. Bernardin may idealise his landscapes by what he chooses to include and omit (rather in the manner of the contemporary neo-classical visual artist), but in what is there one finds no Romantic vagueness or mystification. He is very sparing, in his descriptions, with direct appeals to his readers' subjectivity: even in such dramatic scenes as the two hurricanes we meet only the most occasional and general emotive terms: 'affreux', 'épouvantable' or 'horriblement'. For the rest he works directly with the impressions of a scene on the senses. Finally, nearly all the scenes in the story are the product of a careful stylistic economy and of multiple revision and re-writing, a fact clearly visible from the parallel texts and other materials edited by Marie-Thérèse Veyrenc (2).

The rich opening description reflects all these qualities (pp.81-82). It divides into two equal paragraphs, the one a panorama and the other an account of the small valley basin which was once the home of the families. The only fictional elements in the panorama are this terrain with the cabins and the avenue of bamboos leading to Pamplemousses church. Otherwise it is an economical and scrupulously accurate picture of a real historical scene. If we trace the source of the little river Lataniers on the

map and suppose ourselves looking from a commanding vantage
point (as made explicit at the start of the second paragraph)
along the line of a hill ridge running north by west behind Port-
Louis and with the mountain Le Pouce behind us, then the
details and the orientations are exact. The Baie du Tombeau is,
as the text says, in front of us along the line of the ridge, the path
to Pamplemousses and its church is slightly to our right (north
by east), as are Cap Malheureux and the islands beyond.
Trahard is thus wrong to question the direction of Cap
Malheureux (*1*, p.77, note 1). He also confuses his readers about
the remaining detail, the 'Morne de la Découverte'. This refers
to the signal hill south-west of Port-Louis, whereas La Caille's
map (which Trahard reproduces and to which he refers) shows
only the Piton de la Découverte in the middle of the north of the
island. Indeed, in one draft Bernardin wrote 'à droite' and not 'à
gauche', probably thinking of this peak (*2*, p.230). Both hills
were in fact used for signalling the appearance of ships, and
Bernardin, no doubt eschewing this sort of pedantic
explanation, has opted to mention only the one behind Port-
Louis at this juncture (cf. p.153).

A few more details of maritime history are worth noting. In
the days of sail, ships from West Africa and Europe approached
Mauritius from the east. Off the Cape of Good Hope they
caught the strong westerly winds in the latitude forties (the
Roaring Forties) and some two thousand or so miles later picked
up the south-east trade winds in warmer latitudes to carry them
up the middle of the Indian Ocean towards the island (*20*, pp.86-
94). This is how, contrary to what is stated in our edition's
chronology (p.7), Bernardin himself disembarked on Mauritius
before the military expedition went on to its final destination of
Madagascar. Furthermore, ships from Europe tended to avoid
arriving in the cyclone season (December to April) and few are
on record, especially earlier in the century, as dropping anchor
in December, the month in which the fictional shipwreck occurs.
At any rate, when the *Saint-Géran* appears from the east, this is
entirely normal and not the result of the giant swell (p.154). The
idea that the crew might, under conditions of poor visibility,
mistake the Ile d'Ambre for the Coin de Mire is also to be under-

stood in this context (p.155).

The description of the high valley basin in the next paragraph is a microcosm of Bernardin's technique. Having offered the panorama entirely to our inward eye, he now underlines the elevation and isolation of the position through an explicit appeal to the inward ear: 'les échos de la montagne' and 'le bruit des vents' (p.81). And not forgetting the scale of his panorama, he notes 'le fracas des vagues qui brisent au loin sur les récifs'. The new aural interest thus accompanies the still sustained visual interest: 'les forêts' and 'les récifs'. Thence he proceeds to another contrast: from the noisy solitude of the heights of the vantage point on the crag overlooking the northern exit from the valley, to the silent solitude of the ruined cabins: 'on n'entend plus aucun bruit'. Once in the valley, we are, of course, in a fictional landscape.

Our point of vision is now changed to the 'pied même des cabanes', and colour is introduced for the first time: the rainbow effects from the clouds around the high surrounding crags and then the green and brown of the rock walls leading down from those crags to the spring, source of the Lataniers river. Our eye having been led down, we dwell for an instant on the silence of the valley floor: 'Un silence' and 'A peine l'écho', whence we look up to the valley rim again to see the tops of the palms swaying in the wind. This aspect is retained as the passage concludes with an exclusively visual emphasis on the light of midday contrasting with the colours of gold and purple on the crags at dawn. This last sentence is also a cunning link with the previous panorama. The little valley and the river Lataniers run south-north. In the southern hemisphere the sun moves from east to west but via the north. Only at midday therefore can the lower, northern, part of the valley basin, near its exit, be lit by the sun, which in the Tropics is never very far from being directly overhead at noon. These details are entirely coherent. Yet the critical edition once more risks confusing us, this time by quoting J.-B. Eyriès, who plainly muddles all these orientations and seems to forget which hemisphere he is in (*I*, p.79, note 1)! How clear by contrast is Bernardin and how adept at guiding our imagination with a few deft strokes. He has evoked a whole landscape, indeed sketched a whole geography, in two simple-looking paragraphs. The detail he saves for later in the account of the valley's cultivation by the two families.

Bernardin is lavish with description in terms of the space allotted to it, but he is economical with the species and details which he includes. The *Voyage* is in that sense more richly furnished. An important feature of this self-discipline of the writer is that he mentions comparatively few physical aspects of the island that his characters are not in direct contact and involvement with, particularly in the first half of the narrative. The opening panorama is one obvious case. The next significant set of details, however, appears during the return from the Rivière Noire adventure. This episode lets us glimpse, despite the intervention of the 'good fairy' Providence, the threatening aspects of the island's primeval forests: one can get lost in them and survival skills become important, however briefly. The children eat cress growing in the streams (p.94), and also the fruit of the cabbage-palm, having burnt it down to reach it. The same palm can also supply the material for a shelter (p.96). The hart's-tongue provides Virginie with footwear and bamboo a walking stick. The next specific creatures encountered are the deer (a European introduction), whose call makes Paul hope for help from wandering huntsmen (p.97). Domingue, with the dog, finds them and he makes fire and lights a torch with a twisty green wood (p.98). Finally the outlaw runaways arrive and make a litter of branches and lianas on which to carry the children back home (p.99). Thus Bernardin evokes the threatening quality of untamed nature with extremely sparing detail in its description. Detailed images of truly wild nature appear only later, when the Old Man contemplates it from his solitary homestead in the second part (pp.138-40). In this way Bernardin repeats himself hardly at all, unless it be in the accounts of the two cyclones, one in each half of the story (pp.115-16 and pp.157-59). But in that case the very repetition constitutes local colour: hurricanes are a common feature of Mauritius life. And both accounts relate intimately to the human interest.

This last point is a general truth about all the book's descriptions, even the picture of wild nature just referred to: this accompanies the Old Man's praise of solitude in the second half and is a sensuous expression of that solitude. Thus, although the direct emotional appeal is kept out of the descriptions themselves, the sensuous images offered in them correspond and harmonise with the emotional and human interest prevailing at the time in the story. The landscape is more than merely picturesque, it is part of the children's life. Rich colours, sounds, smells and tactile qualities arise from Paul's landscaping (at the age of twelve) of the valley basin (pp.100-05), and accompany the little community's festivities (pp.109-10). Even where a list of exotic names risks resembling a catalogue, Bernardin manages to fix our imagination with some sensuous quality: '[Paul] allait avec [Domingue] dans les bois voisins déraciner de jeunes plantes de citronniers, d'orangers, de tamarins dont la tête ronde est d'un si beau vert, et d'attiers dont le fruit est plein d'une crème sucrée qui a le parfum de la fleur d'orange' (p.100). After the detail of the landscaping and the species, Bernardin is careful to clinch, in general terms, all the sense impressions of the cultivated valley: 'ces familles se rassemblaient le soir, et jouissaient en silence de la fraîcheur de l'air, du parfum des fleurs, du murmure des fontaines, et des dernières harmonies de la lumière et des ombres' (p.102). Touch, scent, hearing and sight.

The concern for graphic accuracy and clarity shows itself most conspicuously when description is used as one of the terms of a simile, that is, where description and human interest meet directly. The most famous example concerns the children sheltering under Virginie's dress in the rain (p.89). This, interestingly, is the only visual evocation of the children at age six to ten. There are five manuscript versions of it, indicating an intense desire to get it right (*1*, pp.cxxxv-cxxxvii). Virginie's billowing dress covering herself and Paul from a shower is likened to the shell, which, in mythology, enclosed the children of Leda. The descriptive terms are progressively more precise and appropriate in this watery context: 'couverture', 'parapluie' and 'coquille'. The eighteenth-century reader would have had the further advantage of familiarity with the mythological picture, a cultural image clarifying the comparison still further.

Other similes concern not the appearance of the children but their inner life and feelings: their common upbringing is likened to the grafting of different cuttings onto one tree (pp.87-88), the way Virginie's voice reduces Paul's anger resembles the effect of the sun bringing down ice from a mountain top (p.127). The list is not exhaustive and other examples will emerge in other contexts.

Local colour, or allusion to the life and customs of the island, is a second potent feature of the setting's appeal. To this is added, for us, the historical aspect: the past is 'another country' and in that sense doubly exotic. While certain details reflect the real colony which Bernardin knew in 1768-70, for instance the cruelty of plantation owners (pp.93 and 98) and the avidity of colonial traders (p.123), there is also conspicuous idealisation of the cabin life of the families and of the behaviour of the outlaw slaves encountered by the children. The contemporary agronomist, Arthur Young, for whom progress is the equivalent of good business exploitation, presents, in his account of La Bourdonnais's achievement as governor (1735-46), a much less rosy view of the early Ile de France:

> He found it in as miserable a condition as ever colony was; very thin of people, and those ignorant, lazy, and seditious, as if they had not been, as they really were, naked, defenceless and starving. He sent for young negroes over from Madagascar, bred them up in honest and religious principles, and then made use of them against some outlaws and banditti, that were in the island, whom he obliged either to submit, or quit it. He found in the island scarce a planter, manufacturer, or soldier. When he came there was nothing but cabins.[1]

La Bourdonnais's own account of his activities, as reflected by Filliot (*20*, p.58), shows a similar attitude: there was no hope of development without a good importation of slaves, since there was no hope of a good day's work out of idle white inhabitants.

[1] Young, A., *Letters concerning the present state of the French nation* (London, W. Nicoll, 1769), pp.73-74.

Bernardin by contrast, in the eleventh letter of the *Voyage*, sees the corruption of the whites as a recent development, not as an early problem rectified by La Bourdonnais (*3*, pp.108-15).

The principal vehicle of idealisation in *Paul et Virginie* is the figure of the Old Man, the philosopher and sage who suddenly appears from out of the mass of white riff-raff. The idealisation is an integral part of Bernardin's stance against the colonial type of economy and its defenders, and of his views on the natural world. It is not in contradiction with his accuracy of observation and his unique and original powers of evocation: it is the vital force behind them.

2. In What Sense a Novel?

As inheritors of the great nineteenth-century tradition of the
novel, we can easily be taken in by the definite article: how does
Paul et Virginie match up to our demands of *the* novel? The
archetype of this sort of criticism is found in E.M. Forster (see
21), full of sharp insights concerning the kind of fiction which he
knew and practised, but working with the absurd hypothesis that
all the novelists of the universe, past and present, might be
gathered in one seminar to decide the standards of the genre.

Three elements are still in the mainstream of our expectations
of novels: story, plot and people or characters. (It is understood
that animal characters in fiction are usually portrayed with
human traits.) Story arouses our interest for what happens next,
while plot satisfies our wish to know the causal connection of the
events narrated. For story, curiosity is sufficient. Plot also
requires our intelligence and the memory of previous
happenings, so that we may make connections and establish the
reason why. Story is indispensable, laying down a chronological
continuity which allows the reader to orientate himself. It is, as
it were, a basic bodily function of novels, permitting them to live
and, maybe to rise to the nobler heights of plot and characterisation. People are the very heart of a novel's interest and there
are two basic modes of characterisation: 'flat' characters and
'round' characters. A 'flat' character is an embodiment of a
dominant characteristic or 'humour', behaving entirely pre-
dictably according to its type; while a 'round' character 'is
capable of surprising in a convincing way' (*21*, p.106).

This very summary sketch of basic concepts already suggests
how badly *Paul et Virginie* might fare when set against their
measure. For long stretches of the tale nothing very much
happens at all, at least if we understand 'happening' in terms of
events and action: our curiosity for story is disappointed, one
could argue, throughout the idyll (pp.99-113), as well as in the

dialogue of the second half (pp.141-53). In the first case we have descriptions of locations and details of family habits, summer and winter, picnics by the sea and mothers' name-days, while in the second we might consider ourselves outside fiction altogether and in the realm of philosophic dialogue. Even where something does happen, the events may appear disjointed: the quick sketch of the children's early life (pp.87-90) is followed by the receipt of the great-aunt's first letter (pp.90-92). We move on from there to the Rivière Noire adventure, which seems arbitrary and unconnected with what precedes it. For the next set of incidents we have to wait until after the descriptions of the little valley community for the account of events leading to Virginie's departure (pp.113-28). In the second half, incident is even scarcer: Virginie's letter (pp.131-34), her return and shipwreck (pp.153-60) and her funeral and apotheosis (pp.161-62).

If we seek a plot or a framework of causation we can be still further perplexed. Indeed, the question 'why?' hardly seems sensible at all until the account of Virginie's departure. For example, the presence of the two families in the valley and the pattern of their lives are hardly matters requiring subtle explanation. And if we examine Virginie's departure itself, we are likely to be critical, since no clear-cut account of its causes is given. It seems that we are being invited to choose for ourselves between Mme de la Tour's ambitions, the priest's and La Bourdonnais's influence, Virginie's sense of her duty, and the great-aunt's threat of force if she is not obeyed. At any race, all these factors, mixed up together and undifferentiated, seem to be present, as well as a sense that the youngsters ought to be separated for a while anyway. And in the second half is a central event, over which much ink has been spilt in the effort to explain: Virginie's fatal refusal to undress on the ship in order to save herself. Since these are vital moments of the story, the failure to make the patterns of causation clear seems to be a serious weakness.

Matters seem little more promising in the third essential area: characterisation. Clearly the characters are 'flat': they are creatures whose behaviour can nearly always be predicted from what they are. Virginie is the paragon, Paul the impulsive youth and dutiful son by turns, Marguerite on occasion reacts with the down-to-earth attitudes of the peasant woman, while Mme de la Tour, when she is not emulating Marguerite as a model mother, reverts to some of the standpoints of her class. La Bourdonnais, oddly enough, is the one figure who steps out of his role as a type representing corrupt European and colonial values, when suddenly he is made to reflect to Paul on the difficulties of men of power in his position (p.120). This strikes us as a platitude, perhaps, since it is so like the oft-repeated observations of the Old Man, yet it has that element of convincing surprise which goes with roundness of character. He is, however, as the one historical real-life figure to be portrayed in the story, the small exception which proves the rule. Bernardin is almost duty-bound by the living legend of the famous governor to ennoble his character in this way. He is not wicked, whatever Trahard says (*8*, p.130). At most, he and the priest are misguided in their advice (*10*, p.256).

We are accustomed, even with the famous 'flat' characters of a Dickens or an H.G. Wells, to be offered a reasonable amount of physical description in their presentation. With Bernardin's 'flat' characters there is very little, and any physical features mentioned are strictly a function of idealisation. The image of Virginie at the age of twelve is our abiding picture of her, even when she is shipwrecked six years later:

> Virginie n'avait que douze ans; déjà sa taille était plus qu'à demi formée; de grands cheveux blonds ombrageaient sa tête; ses yeux bleus et ses lèvres de corail brillaient du plus tendre éclat sur la fraîcheur de son visage: ils souriaient toujours de concert quand elle parlait; mais quand elle gardait le silence, leur obliquité naturelle vers le ciel leur donnait une expression d'une sensibilité extrême, et même celle d'une légère mélancolie. (p.90)

These characteristics are strikingly general: even the fetching skyward glance in her beautiful blue eyes is less a mark of individuality than a period trait out of the paintings of Greuze. There are no birthmarks, no idiosyncratic angles of chin or fore-

In What Sense a Novel? 27

head which might make of this creature an individual person. Little more is added to this portrait when she appears later in European dress, apart from a high colour and a tremor of emotion in her voice, both a result of her love for Paul (p.123).

Paul is dark where Virginie is blond, the epitome in fact of the tall, dark and handsome youth (p.90). Bernardin's approach to the presentation of both children would thus seem to cast them as creatures of fairy-tale: Virginie is the beautiful princess and Paul her handsome prince. If we consider their mothers, there is even less physical description. We can only infer their qualities from those of their children and from what we know of their social origin. We are told that Mme de la Tour has a 'théologie douce' and Marguerite a 'gaieté vive' (p.107). From this our imaginations might construe that the former is a willowy blond and Marguerite coarser-boned and dark.

With all these figures there is so little characterisation that it hardly seems appropriate to use the word at all. And since the same, to almost the same degree, can be said of story and plot, we seem to be forced to the conclusion that *Paul et Virginie* is fairly paltry stuff as a novel. Indeed, in these three crucial respects the term scarcely seems to apply. Yet Bernardin himself used the word *roman* and generations of critics have called it a masterpiece (7, p.198). Could it be that, with our generally accepted criteria of 'the novel', we are looking in the wrong direction and are not sufficiently receptive to the huge variety of creative possibilities which is open to us in fiction?

The word *roman* has an ambiguity peculiar to the French language, particularly when applied to the eighteenth century, a time when traditional and more experimental forms of fiction are practised side by side. It might, as in the expression 'roman à la mode' used by the Old Man (p.131), refer to the more 'realist' type of fiction portraying the corruption of (high) society as it exists, a sub-genre which is more conspicuously the ancestor of modern fictional practices than some of its contemporaries. It might, however, also be applied more in the sense of 'romance' to any fiction having at its centre an idealised love-interest. In that acceptation it could reach back from Rousseau's *Julie, ou La Nouvelle Héloïse*, via the fiction of *préciosité* in the seventeenth century, to the verse romances of the Middle Ages. The notion of the love-interest is the common core of all these and survives, for instance, in the modern expression 'vivre un roman d'amour'. This last example leads us to a further usage in ordinary language, already current in the eighteenth century: *roman* as the equivalent of pure fantasy or chimera.

These various semantic possibilities are part of the reason for Bernardin's hesitancy over what he is to call his little work. They compound the difficulty which he already has in attaching a label to what he knows very well is original. Thus in a draft of a letter, before publication, he observes to his unknown correspondent: 'Ce roman renferme le résultat de toute ma philosophie' (*5*, p.178 and *6*, pp.236-37), a statement with implications which will emerge later. Yet in the *Avant-propos*, he distances himself from the concept: 'il ne m'a point fallu imaginer de roman pour peindre des familles heureuses' (p.177). This is to be no fantasy. By 1806, secure in the international success of *Paul et Virginie*, he feels confident enough to make huge claims for what he has achieved: 'Plût à Dieu', he observes of his critics, 'qu'ils fussent persuadés que mes *Etudes* sont des romans comme *Paul et Virginie*! Les romans sont les livres les plus agréables, les plus universellement lus, et les plus utiles. Voyez l'*Iliade* et l'*Odyssée*' (p.41). The amusing exaggeration in the comparison is likely to make us overlook its significance: Bernardin understands the worth of fiction in terms of his hopes of living up to an ideal of the great Classical tradition. Indeed, the item originally published with *Paul et Virginie* as the fourth volume of the third edition of the successful *Etudes* is the only completed fragment of a huge epic project: *L'Arcadie*. Though *Paul et Virginie* is not set in the ancient world, as is *L'Arcadie*, it is connected to the older fictional tradition stretching back into the ancient world, and indeed to a specific aspect of that tradition: 'Le thème des amants inséparables dans la vie comme dans la mort, mais sauvés par la mort de l'inévitable flétrissure de vivre: Pyrame et Thisbé, Roméo et Juliette' (*7*, p.177). Bernardin's choice of a title indicates his sense of belonging to this literary family. He does not finally adopt it until the last draft of the text (around 1785), having in the early versions called it *Histoire de Mlle Virginie de la Tour.* Thus we move from a style of title typical of the eighteenth century to a more ancient type, and this change occurs alongside others which increase the factor of idealisation.

These reflexions contain a fundamental indication about genre: they suggest that everything in the text should be read as contributing, or having to contribute, to the picture of the relationship of love between hero and heroine. This is our point of reference for making sense of the basic concepts of story, plot and characterisation, and it should be the central criterion in our assessment of the details of the work. We need, for example, to modify our notion of story, that is, our curiosity to know what comes next, in order to focus not, as is usually the case in a narrative of adventures, upon actions and incidents, but upon new revelations and manifestations concerning the lovers' feelings for each other. The narrative, as it has begun, invites our curiosity in some such terms as 'And then? What else can you tell us about these people and the happiness they once found?' (cf. p.82). Thus the Rivière Noire adventure appears, on a prosaic assessment, to be an attempt to inject some action after the section about the great-aunt, to underscore Virginie's philanthropy and, on the return journey, to show off some knowledge of the flora and fauna and some survival skills. It is actually the point at which the adolescents begin to fall in love and to perceive each other as something other than children. Or rather this is the first time we have been shown them in action in a condition which we have already been told of at the end of the initial sketch of their early lives. Virginie's figure is more than half developed; Paul is taking on the character of a man: 'à leurs regards qui cherchaient à se rencontrer, à leurs sourires rendus par de plus doux sourires, on les eût pris pour ces esprits bien-heureux dont la nature est de s'aimer' (p.90). And lest we be in any doubt about the nature of these feelings (brother and sister do not habitually seek to exchange loving looks), the next words of the text are: 'Cependant Mme de la Tour, voyant sa fille se développer avec tant de charmes, sentait augmenter son inquiétude avec sa tendresse'.

The Rivière Noire adventure, therefore, shows us the

adolescents alone together for the first time. We interpret their
actions and their words on this occasion in terms of the relationship already established. Concerning their attempts to find their
way home and in particular the river crossing, Bernardin strikes
a nice balance between telling and showing, the two chief
strategies of the rhetoric of fiction (*22*, pp.3-20). We are told of
Paul's courage: 'Paul, qui ne s'étonnait de rien', and then
shown the source of it in his words to Virginie: 'N'aie pas peur,
je me sens bien fort avec toi' (p.95). There is sensuality and
purity at the same time in the image of the heroine being carried
on Paul's back. We delight in its innocent ambiguity. 'Allons,
marchons, mon amie' Paul says, and not 'ma sœur', while on
the next page the narrator tells us he is 'chargé de sa sœur'.
Bernardin's comments on Girodet's illustration of this scene for
the 1806 edition leave no doubt about its interpretation. Clearly
any appreciation of this episode must take account of what the
author thought was important about it: 'La confiance de son
amante, qui le presse de ses bras, semble naître ici, pour la
première fois, du courage de l'amant' (p.47).

The scene's 'relevance' is in terms of the real and essential
plot: the growth and development of love. The 'story' is that of
feeling and of a relationship. The fundamental binary structure
of the book also reflects this truth: the first half is the innocent
presence and togetherness of hero and heroine in their valley
home; the second tells of the experience of absence, pain and the
inevitable contact with values inimical to their happiness. There
will be occasion to pursue these thoughts further. For the
moment we may summarise the argument so far as follows: it is
safe to call *Paul et Virginie* a novel, provided that we do not
apply to it criteria foreign to its particular way of being a novel,
to its particular genre. Nothing, of course, prevents us from
expressing distaste for the genre, if we so wish.

Bernardin in fact describes his story more frequently as a
pastorale than as a novel: in the *Avant-propos* as 'une espèce de
pastorale' (p.177); in the *Avis* of 1789 as 'cette pastorale'
(p.180); and in the *Préambule* of 1806 also as 'cette pastorale'
(p.28). This appellation he applies retrospectively to his piece,
though just before its publication, in a letter of 1787 (*6*, p.236).

In Fabre's words: 'il avait écrit une pastorale sans le savoir!' (*7*, p.192). The point is important, since, though Bernardin may be steeped in the kind of reading which feeds his bucolic imagination, the creative energy for the text derives from his marriage of the theme of the doomed lovers to the living land-scape of the island and to the historical reality of the shipwreck. It is a response to experience rather than a literary construct achieved by conscious imitation. He finds that he has respected nearly all the rules, formulated by Florian in 1788, without really trying. In a rule-conscious age, Florian's *Essai sur la pastorale* (published as a preface to his own *pastorale*, *Estelle*) provides Bernardin with a genre pigeon-hole in which to place a work which he did not himself quite know what to make of.

The *pastorale*, as conceived by Florian and his immediate pre-decessors, had become a genre exclusively of prose fiction. In modern terms, therefore, it is a sub-species of the novel largely confined to the late eighteenth century. It is sensible to judge Bernardin's achievement in *Paul et Virginie* in terms of this sub-species to which he explicitly assigned it. In so doing, we find that he more than lived up to its aspirations. Most obviously, concerning pure content, he did what Florian thought of but could not quite bring himself to practise: he dispenses with the traditional requirement to take only shepherds as his characters. This kind of detail, however, is less important than what the *pastorale* strives to be as a literary experience. For Florian one of the chief problems of the bucolic genre is to retain the interest and attention of the reader for the (by definition) innocent, simple and essentially unchanging love of the principal pair of characters. Prose fiction offers the best kind of framework for a solution: 'Dans le roman, deux mots suffisent à la liaison. La marche est vite, rapide; on court d'événements en événements, on ne s'arrête qu'à ceux qui intéressent. Les dialogues, les descriptions, les récits, sont entremêlés et délassent les uns des autres. C'est une campagne riante, coupée de ruisseaux, de bois, de collines; le lecteur y marche longtemps sans se fatiguer'. Another imperative, if interest is to be sustained, is unity of action and of place (a contrast this with d'Urfé's *Astrée* from the seventeenth century): 'Tout doit se toucher dans la pastorale. Le monde finit pour [les bergers] à une lieue de leur village'. The aptness of these remarks if applied to Bernardin is striking. So also is Florian's hope of being morally useful thanks to 'le tableau touchant des mœurs de la campagne, les descriptions toujours agréables des beautés de la nature'.

The opinion that the *pastorale* should moralise is not universally held by its eighteenth-century French practitioners. Marmontel, for example, in his contribution to the article *églogue* of the *Encyclopédie*, thought that it should not. Gessner and Florian take the opposite view, and they are to some extent in reaction against one of the most famous pastoral works of the ancient world, Longus's *Daphnis and Chloë*. This is a frank celebration of nascent sexuality, as the adolescent love of goatherd and shepherdess is followed from its reticent beginnings to its final consummation. As their relationship develops, the pair are placed in situations quite intolerable to eighteenth-century imaginations nurtured on the decencies of *bienséance*. This view of the seemly also informs *Paul et Virginie*.

However, the most interesting aspect of Florian's little sketch of theory, and a relatively neglected one, is his aspiration, in the *pastorale*, towards poetry and lyricism. The neglect is no doubt due in part to the recommendation which expresses this aspiration: Florian would have the pastoralist intersperse his narrative with short passages of verse, preferably in popular idiom. We can indeed be grateful that Bernardin did not have this idea himself, although at least one of his English translators did (cf. *10*, p.250). Great aspirations can sometimes come out as a whimper. If we look away from what Florian recommends to what he admires, we understand his aspiration rather better: prose fiction is only a second best after what Thomson's *Seasons* have achieved in verse, linking, 'jusqu'aux accents les plus sublimes de la poésie', rich descriptions of landscape with the dialogue and actions of shepherd lovers: 'Le roman, après le poème, peut se lire avec intérêt'. Thomson, for Florian, is particularly admirable in his unity of tone. What, however, is meant by 'poésie'? The answer appears in the course of a comparison of Gessner, the Swiss-German pastoralist, with Virgil: 'Gessner n'a pas cette poésie enchanteresse qui ennoblit dans

Virgile les détails les plus communs: il ne charme pas toujours l'oreille comme le poète romain'. 'Poésie', to Florian, means verse: 'Un grand avantage du roman pastoral, c'est le mélange de la poésie et de la prose', and the advantages of verse according to the comparison are twofold: first, to ennoble a subject through a tone; and secondly, to 'charm the ear' through lyricism. Florian is too much a creature of his age to state categorically that prose itself should strive to be poetic and lyrical, or to make the critic's commonplace a reality: 'tirer de la flûte champêtre des sons touchants et harmonieux'.

Bernardin, in prose, actually achieves what Florian only dreams of. His language is noble and preserves a unity of tone, and he attains to a poetic use of prose both through the overall design and through the detail. It is the task of the following chapters to explore this achievement feature by feature. Before proceeding, however, we should note that Florian prizes one quality which we have seen to be prominent in *Paul et Virginie*, namely clarity and precision: 'Vous choisissez les mots les plus simples, les plus clairs, les plus expressifs, pour bien rendre votre tableau. La prose vous donne la facilité de serrer, de presser votre style'. Florian could hardly guess how these virtues were to be wedded to poetry and a new kind of lyricism in an original prose idiom.

3. Elegiac Voices

An analysis of fictional form does well to begin with the mode of narration and the relationship of the author to what he creates. *Paul et Virginie* has two first-person narrators: a persona, or mask, of the author, who conducts the opening description and meets and introduces the chief narrator, the Old Man (pp.81-82). Vivienne Mylne's short and lucid discussion of these figures sets them in the context of the history of fictional techniques, underlining in particular the step towards nineteenth-century practices which the Old Man represents: he tends to be less involved in the action he relates than most of his first-person ancestors, and he displays an omniscience about the characters he portrays more characteristic of the third-person narrator (*10*, pp.246-49). Moreover, Bernardin shows considerable skill in bouncing us into accepting that the Old Man might know things which 'realistically' he cannot. Or, to put it in Booth's terms, the Old Man's narrative 'privilege' of knowing things by other than natural means is rendered extremely unobtrusive (*22*, p.160).

The emphasis of the present chapter, however, will be on the role of these narrators in establishing and maintaining a tone of elegy or lament. For this purpose, it is a particular advantage to have the first narrator meet the second in the very place to which the story refers: the high valley basin. Moreover, by Bernardin's rhetorical art the reader is situated in this location before either narrator is identified. Initially, indeed, we could believe ourselves in a purely third-person form and without any 'dramatised narrator' at all (*22*, p.153). Not only is the opening panorama admirably clear and accurate, it is also the vehicle of a pure elegiac mood: from the first sentence on, the notion of the ruined cabins colours the whole scene emotionally, and the second paragraph describing the high valley stresses the contrast between the melancholy silence of the floor of the enclosure and the distant noise of wind in the trees and breakers on the reefs.

Before we have any people, even the narrators, we have a
desolate place and a melancholy solitude. This is to be an elegy
in a Mauritius valley.

The appearance of the authorial first person (p.82) comes as a
slight jolt, because now there is suddenly a dramatised narrator
where before there was merely generalised melancholy and solitude, because suddenly the aesthetic enjoyment, which has been
exclusively the reader's, is attributed to this new figure:
'J'aimais à me rendre dans ce lieu'. This remark begins the
sequence leading to the meeting with the Old Man, whose reply
to the authorial narrator's curiosity makes the elegiac register
specific: what European would want to know about the people
who once lived here? Then, at the first narrator's insistence, the
story proper begins. The function of the 'frame', that is, the
opening description and those parts of the text where the two
narrators address each other, is thus principally an elegiac one.
It keeps a desolate present before out eye as a backcloth to a
golden past. This happens, however, not only in the explicit
'frame', that is, the beginning and end, and the breaking-off of
the narrative in the middle (p.128), but also in repeated regretful
comments by the Old Man comparing the past with the
melancholy present, and in explicit or oblique references to the
place where the *viva voce* narration is happening: for example,
the Old Man's home is 'à une lieue et demie d'ici' (p.136). (The
lieue, or league, is roughly five kilometres.) The tearful
comments and the sustained sense of place ensure that the
elegiac atmosphere is never disrupted. The setting is high up in
the hills, and this, in Bernardin's own sensibility, implies both
melancholy and flight from the world and the attempt to rise
above conflict by the force of reflexion: 'La bonté m'attire dans
la vallée', he observes in the manuscript draft *Sur mon caractère*
(c. 1790), 'et le malheur me fait réfugier dans la montagne' (*6*,
p.153). Melancholy and tears are a part of our rising above the
daily round and the ambitions we share with our fellow men.
The elevation of the setting anticipates the elevation of the
sentiments. And of the tone.

We need to consider the author's stance as artist, therefore,
not in order to connect his biography directly to the events of his

tale, but in order to emphasise the vital connection between the motif of elegy and the *pastorale* as a genre. Friedrich Schiller, the great German dramatist and critic, has given us the perfect instrument for this purpose in his famous essay: *Über naive und sentimentalische Dichtung* (*On the naive and the 'sentimental' in literature*) (1795). This work has the advantage of being very nearly contemporary, and, although it nowhere refers to *Paul et Virginie* directly, notions of the elegiac and the idyllic bulk large in its argument.

Naive poets (great examples are Homer and Shakespeare) succeed, by the force of creative genius, in portraying human nature 'as it is', without any sense of nostalgia or of reflective commentary, overt or implied. They are nowhere visible for us to discourse with behind their texts. The text, with the nature it sets forth, is all there is. The 'sentimental' poet, by contrast, is always caught between a human actuality which cannot be denied and his ideas or aspirations on behalf of humanity, which are in principle limitless: his eye is always on these two things at once, and the mixed feelings which he arouses testify to the fact. To the 'sentimental' writer the natural is always ideal, not an immediate lived reality presented in the writing. Here we have then a strictly technical use of the terms 'naive' and 'sentimental'.

The 'sentimental' mode of writing is either 'satirical', that is, it contrasts human actuality with the highest reality as falling short of the ideal; or it is 'elegiac', concentrating not on the difference of the actual from the ideal, but on the ideal itself. Nature and the ideal are an object of sadness if nature is treated as lost and the ideal as unattained. This is elegy in the narrow sense. Or both nature and the ideal are represented as actual and become an object of joy. This is the idyll in the broader sense. All these various terms refer to the artist's mode of perceiving his material, to his literary stance, to 'genre' in the broad and not the narrow sense. They can each apply to such things as the epic, the tragedy, etc.

If elegy laments the loss of an ideally perfect nature which has never existed, idyll rather represents man in a state of innocence, that is, in a condition of harmony and peace with himself and with his environment. In practice the idyll usually takes the form of portraying man as he was (notionally and ideally) at the beginnings of civilisation. Schiller has high ambitions for the idyll as he understands it, and takes it extremely seriously. The harmony which it seeks is to be found not only in a retreat from the corruptions of civilisation but also in victory over them. The 'sentimental' poet's art, at its best, is a mark of indomitable human spirit and a constant encouragement to human striving.

Such ideas, of course, embrace the whole field of literature and it remains to be seen how far Bernardin, in his small corner of the universe of letters, measures up to such aspirations. Nevertheless, they help us appreciate the essential gravity of the concepts of the elegiac and the idyllic. Above all we should note, in reference to Bernardin, that elegy in the narrow sense and idyll in the broader sense both belong to the elegiac stance of the writer. Both suppose a gulf between the ideal which the artist seeks and the actuality within which he stands. Even when the 'sentimental' creator offers us the picture of the harmony of the idyll, he does so knowing that it is ideal: nature not as it is but as it should be. Even the portrayal of harmony contains the regret that it is only an idea.

In this broad sense therefore, *Paul et Virginie* is 'elegiac'. More narrowly, it is elegiac in its intrinsic melancholy, reflecting Bernardin's prevailing mood in the difficult years of its creation, 1771-85. It is a 'poem from the heart'. However, the use of the two narrators allows him to distance himself from his own mood, from his own emotional need, and to shape and control it artistically. The authorial narrator, both before and after he is 'dramatised' by appearing as a 'Je', is austere, permitting himself to mention his own tears only in the very last lines of the text. Elegy (in the narrow sense) is established in the opening description through the kind of scene we are shown, but it is only the Old Man who tells of the sadness by striking an explicit lamenting note. The authorial narrator is even initially distanced from the specific human story which must lie behind the ruined cabins, because he takes aesthetic delight in the melancholy of the place, and in its picturesque features. Thus we have another function for this shadowy first narrator, apart from the establishment of the sense of place: a degree of distancing from the author.

The choice of the Old Man as principal narrator is an obvious one, indeed a necessary one given the chronology. The conversation with the authorial figure is deemed to happen some twenty years after the shipwreck (p.82); and we must add almost another twenty years to that, if he is to witness the arrival in this place of Mme de la Tour, before the birth of Virginie. Thus forty years previously the Old Man must have already travelled the world enough to have sought the retreat which permits him to make the two women's acquaintance. The least he can be, therefore, is around seventy. Yet these details of his life are only provided retrospectively in the second half, a feature which corresponds perfectly with the figure's double role as narrator. His authority is absolute as to the events of the story and he speaks as an omniscient narrator. His other authority, as a moral commentator, comes particularly to the fore in the second half.

At the start of the tale the Old Man eases into the picture very gradually. His voice does not reveal all its resources at once, and is so muted in its entry into the narrative, that for a time we are not sure which voice we are listening to: 'En 1726 un jeune homme de Normandie ...' (p.82). Are these the words of the Old Man or of the first narrator giving an account of what he said? The Old Man pressing his brow as an aid to memory suggests the former. But 'voici ce que ce vieillard me raconta' allows the latter interpretation: 'here is what he told me'. Significantly, in neither the first nor the definitive edition of the text (1788 and 1806) is there any indication from the punctuation that a new voice is actually speaking. Since the introductory dialogue, by contrast, is carefully punctuated, we must take this omission to be deliberate artistic judgment by Bernardin. The initial details about the arrival of the La Tour family in Mauritius are thoroughly prosaic in tone and we are left wondering who utters them.

After four paragraphs we know for sure, as the Old Man comes in with his own 'Je'. An emotional *forte* follows the *pianissimo* entry. This occurs only after two developments in those four paragraphs (a sort of *crescendo*) have increased the emotional intensity: a passage on our instinct for seeking refuge in solitude, and a description of the providential and tearful meeting of the two women. The Old Man introduces himself explicitly, both into the narrative and into the story itself, at points of high emotional intensity and also at points where he can take in the past and the present at a single glance. 'Je connaissais Marguerite, et quoique je demeure à une lieue et demie d'ici, dans les bois, derrière la Montagne-Longue, je me regardais comme son voisin'. Here, as in his first explicit appearance, the note of elegy is dominant, as the contrast of the present with the past is linked to changes in the island's social and economic life: 'Dans ce temps-là surtout, où cette île faisait peu de commerce aux Indes, le simple voisinage y était un titre d'amitié' (p.84).

The Old Man, then, is the elegiac voice *par excellence*. By speaking through this figure Bernardin is able not only to distance himself somewhat as author, but also to give the elegiac register a consistent nobility of tone and to endow it with a degree of authenticity: the ideal figure adopts an appropriate noble language. To this end, Bernardin discourages us from thinking that his narrator, who also takes some part in the action, was ever younger than he seems to be from his narrating voice. A nice indication of this, which critics tend to point out as a slip in technique, is the introduction of the second half dialogue between him and Paul. It would appear that there is to be no punctuation differentiating the two speakers: 'il vous sera aisé de faire la différence des interlocuteurs par le sens de mes questions et de mes réponses' (p.141). (We can note in passing that this is also yet another reminder of the basic narrative situation.) The dialogue is nevertheless punctuated, and, what is more, provided with markers of who speaks, as in a play: 'Le Vieillard' and 'Paul'. Now, their words are deemed to be uttered at least twenty-five years before the basic narrative situation, so one of the speakers is not yet strictly a 'vieillard', not even in an epoch where one moved rather quickly through middle age. So is this an inadvertency by Bernardin, or a deliberate underlining of the authority and elegiac quality of his narrator? That introductory sentence, which seems like a slip, is almost inviting us to take note of how the dialogue is presented.

Because the Old Man is given relatively little to do in the story of the families whose lives he tells, because his chief role is to observe, to comment, and above all to lament, it is possible for us to think of him as always having been old. There are two places where this impression risks breaking down: the first is when he is described as helping the two women to build their huts (p.85), and the second is when he appears to give conflicting advice to the families during the crisis leading to Virginie's departure. The risk in the first case is small until we are told (p.87) that religion helps the women to give up any thoughts of new men in their lives. This is, of course, a highly realistic thought, but perhaps one which it would have been cleverer to omit: if we put two and two together, we realise that this narrator (as he was when he knew the women) was the only likely contender in such a race, certainly the only one that the story allows us to see. Fortunately, few readers, I suspect, make this connection, since the references are rapid and in any case separated by a few pages. The risk in the second case is that of reminding us of the difference between the Old Man of the narrating voice and the (younger) neighbour of the two women by calling into question his judgment as a younger man: at first he favours Paul's departure for India, but is quickly set to rights by Paul's own 'bon sens fort au-dessus de son âge' (p.117). Here again however, there are so many conflicting motives and intentions at this point of the story that it is simply one oscillation among others, and quickly overtaken by the arrival of the great-aunt's second letter. These two cases, then, are slight exceptions proving the rule that Bernardin has narrowed the gap as much as possible between the neighbour who observes and takes some part in the families' lives, and the Old Man who tells us their story. The Old Man hardly ever refers to himself and his own past feelings. To allow this to occur would be to undermine his authority as narrator. This, perhaps, is why we have the impression that this figure is even less involved in the story he tells than on close examination he really is: he is the instrument of the elegy, marking the contrast between the happy past of the families and the desolate present. He is not setting out his own story, although we take it for granted, if the question is put to us, that his life was closely bound up with theirs.

If we do have the latter impression, it is because this particular fictional rhetoric succeeds in convincing us of the Old Man's omniscience. His prestige makes his 'privilege' as narrator seem entirely natural. The Old Man exemplifies another point about Schiller's fundamental distinction between the naive and the 'sentimental': whereas the naive perception works with the individuality of nature, presenting its creatures 'as they are' in their particulars, the 'sentimental' tends towards the ideal and away from the individual. In Bernardin's first draft, the Old Man had a name: M. Mustel, a memory of a real-life Dutch friend. In the final version he has simply the quality which befits his elegiac voice, he is merely the Old Man. A similar process occurs in the case of a much less important character, the missionary priest. Whereas originally Bernardin had practically specified his wickedness with an unpleasant name: Ignou or, alternatively, Higou (*2*, p.281), the printed text leaves him nameless and merely fulfilling the role one might expect from his type. We have already seen too how little individuality the chief characters have, and we tend in terms of our own taste to regard this as a weakness. If Schiller is right, however, we should see it as part of the intrinsic tendency of 'sentimental' literature, particularly in its elegiac and idyllic modes, towards the ideal.

How, in terms of the framework of elegy, are we to assess the oft-repeated contrasts between Europe and the little valley? This motif is already there in the first draft, so we may not argue that it has been introduced later with the increasing didactic emphasis. It is, on the other hand, true that the feature is much more marked in the definitive text. To the extent that references to corrupt Europe bring us firmly into the narrating time, as in the Old Man's direct address to his authorial interlocutor, they are clearly elegiac, stressing how far away from us the idyllic picture is. They are also however, in Schiller's terms, 'satirical', that is, they point us toward criticism of the existing state of society and are not content merely to portray nature as lost and

the ideal as unattained (elegy in the narrow sense). Now, for
Schiller the true source of the 'satirical' is the ideal, the notion of
a reality superior to that which actually exists, that is, it is not
dependent merely on the material needs or secret desires of the
writer.

The 'satirical' strand is clearly visible in *Paul et Virginie*, but it
would appear too important if it were to be given a chapter in its
own right. It will help to place it in perspective if we return to it
briefly in the conclusion, after the major theme of sensibility has
been tackled. The context has now been established for what
follows: human feeling (and not story, plot and characters) is the
stuff of Bernardin's text. And his fundamental stance is elegiac:
he portrays feeling not 'as it is' but 'as it might be'.

4. Sensibility and Morality

On a été sévère pour la sensibilité du XVIIIe siècle, dont on s'est acharné à souligner les démonstrations ridicules. On n'a pas assez dit qu'à travers les effusions et les enthousiasmes s'exprime un immense appétit d'absolu, que les âmes du siècle n'avaient aucun autre moyen d'assouvir. Même la plus insoutenable déclamation peut être une pathétique affirmation de soi, une tentative pour échapper au néant. (*9*, p.513)

This observation is directly relevant to *Paul et Virginie*. Not only are Bernardin's heroes effusive, they inhabit an unfashionable universe governed by Providence and final causes, that is, by a principle of purpose. He incurs thereby a double ridicule. Though our own moral climate is unsympathetic to such notions and to such effusions, I shall try, for the sake of the work's positive literary merits, to present its intellectual framework dispassionately.

It was shrewd commercial judgment to publish the story as a new part of the third edition of the very successful *Etudes de la nature*. But it also implied that the tale in some sense exemplifies the theories of the *Etudes*. To pursue this connection is not to argue that *Paul et Virginie* is a mere illustrative footnote, but rather to counter the received opinion that its intellectual background is inferior rousseauism. The most relevant material for this purpose is found in the twelfth *Etude*, entitled 'De quelques lois morales de la nature. Faiblesse de la raison; du sentiment; preuves de la divinité et de l'immortalité de l'âme par le sentiment'. First, Bernardin makes his own peculiar use of the traditional distinction between our animal and spiritual natures: 'Il y a en l'homme deux puissances, l'une animale et l'autre divine. La première lui donne sans cesse le sentiment de sa misère, la seconde celui de son excellence' (*4*, III, pp.33-34). Our

consciousness (first sense of *sentiment*) of these two natures
manifests itself, in Bernardin's view, in the form of an *élan*
(second sense of *sentiment*) towards refuge and repose in the
case of our weak and fragile animal nature, and towards a trans-
cending movement and activity outside ourselves in the case of
our spiritual nature. Characteristically, he understands happiness as depending on a balance of these two aspirations.

Sentiment is thus at once a manifestation of the soul's energy
and a form of cognition alongside the reason. It is superior to
reason in providing intimations of the absolute. While the
analytic reason divisively sharpens our passions by increasing
our sense of inadequacy, *sentiment* offers the sense of our unity
with an absolute Nature:

> Le sentiment se flatte, au milieu des ruines, des combats et
> de la mort même, de je ne sais quelle existence éternelle; il
> poursuit dans tous ces faits les attributs de la divinité,
> l'infinité, l'étendue, la durée, la puissance, la grandeur et
> la gloire; il en mêle les désirs ardents à toutes nos passions,
> il leur donne ainsi une impulsion sublime; et, en
> subjuguant notre raison, il devient lui-même le plus noble
> et le plus délicieux instinct de la vie humaine. (*4*, III, p.16)

The firm foundation of morality and happiness, and the
guarantee against the risk of anarchy which these lines might
seem to imply, is provided by order and virtue. *Sentiment*, filling
the soul with the sense of its energy when the soul is in the
receptive condition of repose, is the *sine qua non* of happiness
itself, but without order and virtue it is not a sufficient condition.

It is axiomatic for Bernardin that Nature is an ordered system.
However, since it is a transcendent Order, he has some difficulty
in establishing how finite human beings can be reliably in touch
with it. In his view, the Order of Nature, being a series of
relationships of appropriateness with a single common centre,
'pleases' us, that is, it is in tune with our *sentiment*, both by its
vast variety and its essential unity. The two different sides of our
human nature are both satisfied by its contemplation: our

spiritual side, on wings of reason and imagination, can take in the universe in its vastness and diversity, while the conviction of its basic unity is a solace to the weaker side of our nature which seeks refuge and repose. The flaw in this view of the universe is not difficult to find: either the Order is perceptible through the physical world (and it is hard to see how it can be to a finite mind), or it is transcendent, metaphysically out of reach, and not available to the soul's contemplation. Bernardin, who is dealing in analogy and metaphor, does not let this worry him. Yet, though the resulting anthropomorphic view of Nature hardly satisfies the philosopher, it suits the poetic primitivism of *Paul et Virginie* as literature. The heroine's body is found half buried in the sands of the Baie du Tombeau: 'comme si la mer eût voulu rapporter son corps à sa famille, et rendre les derniers devoirs à sa pudeur' (p.175). Even in the thick of disaster, Nature has a human face.

The beauty of *Paul et Virginie* as literature is intimately connected with the rapprochement of *sentiment* and Nature:

> La beauté du roman — encore méconnue dans la plus récente édition — tient au merveilleux accord entre une certaine idée du bonheur et son expression littéraire. Dans ce jardin primitif que l'homme n'a pas gâté, tout parle pourtant le langage de l'homme. Tout est bienveillant et ami. Le "repos de Virginie" exprime cette admirable fusion entre l'âme et les choses. (*9*, p.652)

One should add that this correspondence (*accord*) extends beyond the description of the children's innocent early happiness. It pervades the whole work and reaches its highest expression in the prosopopeia of Virginie, the Old Man's ultimate attempt to console the grief-stricken Paul. The absolute, represented in the recurring motif of 'tout', is understood in terms of sensibility:

> Dans nos souhaits innocents nous désirions être tout vue, pour jouir des riches couleurs de l'aurore; tout odorat, pour sentir les parfums de nos plantes; tout ouïe, pour

entendre les concerts de nos oiseaux; tout cœur, pour reconnaître ces bienfaits. Maintenant à la source de la beauté d'où découle tout ce qui est agréable sur la terre, mon âme voit, goûte, entend, touche immédiatement ce qu'elle ne pouvait sentir alors que par de faibles organes. Tout ce qu'une puissance infinie et une bonté céleste ont pu créer pour consoler un être malheureux; tout ce que l'amitié d'une infinité d'êtres, réjouis de la même félicité, peut mettre d'harmonie dans des transports communs, nous l'éprouvons sans mélange. (pp.170-71)

This is the poetic presentation of Bernardin's own aspiration, in the *Etudes*, to experience the Order of Nature in both its diversity and its essential unity, and to present that experience as what we should call scientific knowledge. He has some quaint and amusing ways of going about this, insisting to the very end that the *Etudes* merit for him an honoured place in the scientific community and scientific institutions of France. Yet at bottom his aspiration is very much of its time: Goethe is not satisfied with an account of colour merely in terms of mathematics and measurement; and, in the opinion of C. Gillispie at least, great Encyclopedists were no less anti-scientific: even the influence of a Diderot, he holds, may be seen as 'reaching into the heart of science to turn it into moral philosophy. We must take this aspect of the Encyclopedic movement of thought not as the expression of a developing scientific culture, but as strictly inimical to scientific culture in effect as in intent'.[2] According to Gillispie, this anti-scientific spirit reached a peak during the Jacobin ascendancy in the French Revolution. The Jacobins, who were later to destroy the great chemist Lavoisier in the Terror, helped to translate Bernardin, as successor to the pioneering natural historian Buffon, to the post of Intendant of the Jardin du Roi (1792-93), which became the Muséum d'Histoire Naturelle during his tenure. In historical terms at

[2] Gillispie, C.C., 'The *Encyclopédie* and the Jacobin philosophy of science: a study in ideas and consequences', in M. Clagett (ed.), *Critical problems in the history of science* (colloquium) (Madison, Wisconsin University Press, 1962), pp.255-89 (p.280).

least therefore, we should take seriously the intellectual aspiration reflected, poetically, in the prosopopeia of Virginie.

Bernardin's own quarrel with the Encyclopedists was over religion and such issues as Providence, not over the desire to treat science and moral philosophy as one. For him the dominant framework of causation in Nature is finality or purpose. The dynamism of Nature's Order is that its diverse elements tend towards their proper condition or place. The 'natural' is thus understood not as what 'is' but rather as what 'ought to be'. The chief imperative governing the dynamism is that of balance, and order is to that extent synonymous, on the cosmic scale, with equilibrium. On the local scale, human *sentiment*, knowingly or unknowingly, aspires to that same balance and is itself therefore always goal-directed and a part of Nature. The modern commentator all too often approaches *Paul et Virginie* with his own strictly realistic understanding of the natural and finds it easy thereby to uncover incoherencies and ambiguities in the text. We mistake the genre of Bernardin's discourse if we assume that the work might be judged as something other than faithful to its own system of final causes and purposes. Without that system as a framework, the novel would not exist: it portrays an anthropomorphic Nature and exemplifies the pathetic fallacy. We regularly enjoy works of art whose intellectual frameworks we would not as such accept. It is probably only Bernardin's overt didacticism which makes us react differently in his case. Nevertheless, we are free to ignore it or to accept it in silence as one of the 'period' features. It is even advisable to do so, if we are to concentrate on the work's considerable positive merits.

The theme of the correspondence of human aspiration and Nature is unproblematic for as long as the children are portrayed in their early and adolescent innocence. The youngsters are so at home in their little valley world that, at the end of the initial rapid sketch of their childhood, their silence at meal times is described in terms pre-figuring the sense of the absolute expressed in the prosopopeia (pp.170-71):

A leurs regards qui cherchaient à se rencontrer, à leurs

sourires rendus par de plus doux sourires, on les eût pris
pour ces enfants du ciel, pour ces esprits bienheureux dont
la nature est de s'aimer, et qui n'ont pas besoin de rendre le
sentiment par des pensées, et l'amitié par des paroles.
(p.90)

Their youth is thus a pure communication of their inner lives
and their affectionate feelings. Sensibility in this sense is their
very mode of existence. It is conspicuous that Bernardin
establishes this mutuality of feeling, person to person, this
climate of sensibility, before he portrays the youngsters' lives
close to the natural world. He does, however, prepare that portrayal with some magnificent similes:

Comme deux bourgeons qui restent sur deux arbres de la
même espèce, dont la tempête a brisé toutes les branches,
viennent à reproduire des fruits plus doux, si chacun d'eux,
détaché du tronc maternel, est greffé sur le tronc voisin;
ainsi ces deux petits enfants, privés de tous leurs parents, se
remplissaient de sentiments plus tendres que ceux de fils et
de fille, de frère et de sœur, quand ils venaient à être
changés de mamelles par les deux amies qui leur avaient
donné le jour. (pp.87-88)

Ainsi se passa leur première enfance comme une belle aube
qui annonce un plus beau jour. (p.89)

Morally, the image of the children's innocent happiness is an
image of spontaneity. They behave well as a function of their
natural impulses. Those impulses and feelings are understood
not as anarchic and individualistic but as goal-directed, harmon-
ising with the ultimate purposes of Nature: the children are
living 'as Nature intended'. The Rivière Noire adventure to
return the runaway slave, before the idyll proper, is already an
illustration, within a framework of spontaneity and innocence,
of the two aspects of human nature: the spiritual, which reaches
out into action, and the animal, which retreats into refuge and
repose. Virginie's impulse to ask for the slave's pardon is as

spontaneous and immediate as an appetite: 'j'ai envie d'aller demander votre grâce' (p.93). (I wonder if white children called slaves 'vous'.) She obeys, so to speak, the divine spark of spiritual energy and moves off with her brother to make the round trip of more than fifty kilometres barefoot.

The episode is thus more than an excuse for some action: it is a portrayal of Virginie's virtuous soul. Since we are in a context of spontaneity, virtue must be equated with the natural. The authorial narrator makes this explicit in inviting the Old Man to tell his tale and mentioning the 'bonheur que donnent la nature et la vertu' (p.82). Two observations may be made on this point. First, this view of virtue is clearly different from Rousseau's, despite the fact that the most conspicuous definition of *vertu* offered in the course of the text is a rousseauistic one: 'un effort fait sur nous-mêmes pour le bien d'autrui dans l'intention de plaire à Dieu seul' (p.150). The context of these words is all-important: there is a need to steel Paul against his deprivation. Secondly, however, the *Préambule* of 1806 suggests an equation of virtue with the ideas of constancy and balance, in terms of both the physical and the moral laws of Nature. Bernardin's chosen motto for himself in that edition is '*Stat in medio virtus, librata contrariis.* "La vertu est stable au milieu, balancée par les contraires."' (p.45). The motto is hardly a model of clarity, but it does permit us to regard the moral law as tending always to equilibrium. Virginie's spontaneous philanthropic impulse, unknown to herself, is a move in the direction of restoring the balance of Nature, disturbed by the cruelties of the slave-owner. Her spontaneous feeling shows the moral law to be operative.

It seems perfectly obvious, in a realist perspective, that the girl's 'spontaneous' act is loaded with social values. It is true that her actual first impulse is to feed the almost naked creature with the household's Sunday lunch. We may wonder why she does not think to clothe her as well, but above all why should she think that returning the slave is a kindness to her? Here again sensibility is dominant: in her innocence Virginie assumes that any human being would, as she does, feel pity for the slave's condition. This is psychologically plausible in the context of the isolated life the children have hitherto led. She might also know that runaways are pursued with savage cruelty and that it is no kindness at all to send the slave on her way after her square meal. However, it is also true that Virginie's act conforms completely to the social code of the colony, which frowns heavily on assisting runaways (one can compare Huckleberry Finn's guilt feelings on helping Nigger Jim).

Such social conventions are not mentioned explicitly, and this fact, coupled with the dependence on slave labour of the little valley community itself, could suggest to the modern reader that the novel condones slavery as an institution. Probably it comes as a surprise, at any rate, to learn that Bernardin, in the *Voyage*, publicly states his abolitionist commitment (*3*, pp.121-22). Nowadays we expect slavery to be condemned outright as soon as it is mentioned. In fact, *Paul et Virginie* makes its own kind of contribution to the anti-slavery cause and Bernardin is not contradicting himself. First, his literary imagination works with the historical reality of the Mauritius he knew, so we can hardly blame him for making Marguerite and Mme de la Tour slave-owners. He had, after all, owned two slaves himself during his stay (called César and Pompée!). His conventional eighteenth-century claim that the novel is a true story simply reinforces this point. Secondly, however, his imagination clearly transfigures that historical reality, not least in the picture which it projects of black people: one finds no wicked or objectionable blacks in his tale. The contrast is particularly stark between his idealised vision of the grateful band of runaways and the threat which such outlaws had undoubtedly posed to the settled life of the island. We perceive something of that threat in the ruthlessly practical view adopted by apologists of colonial trade such as La Caille, La Bourdonnais and, in England, Arthur Young. These writers see runaways as little better than a predatory vermin to be exterminated by any possible means.

Paul et Virginie, a work of imaginative literature, serves the cause of black people, not by fulminating against the institution of slavery, but through its appeal to positive emotions. Throughout the book there is a stress on the common humanity of black and white: in the domestic picture of the two adjacent households and more actively in the Rivière Noire adventure. It is easily forgotten that the institution of slavery tends to deny such common humanity and to reduce the slave to the level of a non-person. In an age when some educated readers (even some social reformers of the Enlightenment) hardly thought about blacks as people at all, Bernardin's insistence on their sensibilities subverts the unthinking assumptions which underpin the slave system.

If the journey to the Rivière Noire is a mark of Virginie's instinctive virtue and of the individual's active reaching out to conquer a moral world beyond herself, then the return journey is very much a portrait of the children's vulnerability and yearning for the refuge of home. The whole adventure is, as it were, an active demonstration of Bernardin's theory of the two sides of human nature. Yet while Virginie's philanthropic impulse and the subsequent weakness of the children in the context of wild nature is the explicit theme of the episode, the concrete imagery of the scene conveys its implicit theme: the first stirrings of love as the boy strives to rescue the girl and the girl entrusts herself to his attempts to do so. Bernardin's approval of Girodet's illustration of the scene of the river crossing leaves no doubt as to this interpretation (p.47). The chief plot element of this episode and of the idyll which follows it (pp.92-113) is the opening out of this nascent love in all its innocence. This is, so to speak, the 'logic' of the rhythm of the idyll: Paul's landscaping, description of which begins as a flashback, culminates in the 'repos de Virginie' and in the suggestion, thanks to the final embellishments, that the landscaping efforts are all in the end for the sake of Virginie (p.105). Their (as yet) unavowed love is inseparable from its setting in a beneficent Nature.

This atmosphere established, the accounts of the families' winter and summer activities are conducted with a more familiar kind of sensibility. There are many opportunities for tears as they listen to stories of adventure or stories from the Bible, and as they engage in philanthropic work. The unalloyed joys of the summer picnics, and in particular the mimed and danced representations by the children of some famous love stories, prepare, with the brief interlude concerning the mothers' name-days, for the high point of their innocent affection: the 'love-

duet' (pp.112-13). Spontaneous happiness at one with Nature is
thus the central motif of the idyll, although it does not preclude
the sense of a progression. Up to this point their morality,
indeed their whole life, is their sensibility.

A change occurs as Virginie begins to become aware of the
physical transformations of adolescence. These appear in the
narrative as following the phase of innocent love, though
logically they are a flashback: 'depuis quelque temps' (p.113).
Bernardin has adjusted his chronology in order to portray the
adolescents' innocence as an undivided unity aside from the
physical manifestations of sexuality. We are aware at this point
in the narrative, if we were not already, that Bernardin, throughout the idyll, has exploited an ambiguity between the brother/
sister relationship on the one hand and the growing relationship
as lovers on the other. The expressions of affection, words,
kisses, tears, exclamations of mutual praise and of grief, the
physical contact of the scene of the crossing of the torrent
(pp.95-96), in all of these a kind of dramatic irony operates in
which we know more about the children's condition than they
do. By the treatment of the youngsters as brother and sister their
nascent love is made to look as if it belonged to the golden
mythical age of Saturn's reign, when, to use Milton's words,
'such mixture was not thought a stain'. At the same time their
'incestuous' affection is only notionally so, since they are not
brother and sister in blood. The fascination of a time preceding
the taboo is preserved, while at the same time modern conventional morality is respected. This ambiguity is one of the
powerful charms of the idyll. Its ultimate expression is the comparison of the adolescents to Adam and Eve in the Garden of
Eden, who are one flesh (closer than brother and sister) and
whose initial relationship is without passion and without any
excess or depravity (p.112).

Passion enters the picture of the relationship of Paul and
Virginie precisely at the point where the girl begins to be sexually
aware. Here passion is understood in its classic sense of an
influence arising from the animal spirits and tending to take
control of behaviour away from the conscious will. For
Bernardin the word describes a situation in which impulse and

will are no longer in spontaneous harmony but rather conflict. Virginie is oppressed by the struggle within herself between her affection for her 'brother' and the new unfamiliar impulses of sexuality (pp.113-14). Almost at once, Bernardin employs the description of overpowering summer heat in order to convey this sense of oppression (p.114). Once again there is intimate correspondence between the moods of Nature and of the human beings. The dramatic power of the scene of Virginie's midnight bathe lies partly in her failure to find solace in the very place where, up to now, it has always been — in the bosom of Nature. For the first time we see her immerse herself in the waters of her 'repos' which are also the source of all life in the valley. The prosaic sense is that she is trying to cool herself down, but symbolically this is an unsuccessful attempt to return to unity with Nature (her mind is at this point full of memories of innocent times). The new, natural forces within her make the old easy relationship with Nature impossible, and she is forced to flee from her new self to her mother for comfort (p.115). Virginie, in her sexuality, is caught up by the animal side of her nature which gives rise to the sense of weakness and the desire for retreat.

Spontaneity is now no longer the rule of morality: the advent of sexuality is likened, by juxtaposition, to the storm which devastates the valley garden landscaped by Paul, including, most importantly of all, Virginie's 'repos' (p.116). Its destruction is a symbol of vanished innocence. Virginie's reflexion on the sad scene could be applied to her own development: 'il n'y a que le ciel qui ne change point' (p.116). The appearance of sexuality is a change occurring according to the inexorable laws of Nature. However, the appearance of the impulse is one thing, its proper destination and purpose is another. It is facile to regard all the barriers to the adolescents' instant marriage as artificial and the product of European prejudice. When Marguerite proposes their immediate union, it is in a spirit of weakness in order to forestall the moment when the commanding voice of sex speaks to Paul (p.117). Mme de la Tour's rejection of the proposal is on two counts: the one is their poverty, but the other (not a social reason this) is that they are too young. Virginie is twelve and Paul therefore thirteen. The first draft of the text made this

explicit with a precise date (*2*, p.267). The removal of the precise
date does not mean that the basic chronology has been changed.
It can be deduced from the indications given (pp.111, 114 and
118). We could argue purely on health grounds that the children
should be separated. Certainly, still by the standards of the
nineteen-eighties, it is reasonable for Mme de la Tour to insist
that they should not marry at this age.

The point at issue here morally is in the end whether the
children can yet be responsible for their own future. Plainly, on
the question of sex and marriage they need their elders to see
what is in their best interests. The delay in their union does not
mean that the mothers have given up their intention to marry
them, even when the great-aunt's fortune and wishes become
known. It is quite wrong, therefore, to construe Mme de la
Tour's wish to delay the event as disingenuous prevarication,
hoping that something better will come along. These are merely
the understandable inferences drawn by Paul, particularly when
he sees that secrets are being kept from him.

In the chaos of intention and counter-intention generated by
the need to separate the children from each other, the concept of
virtue takes on a key importance. For the first time we can
properly apply the rousseauistic definition made explicit in the
second half: Virginie needs to make an effort of will to keep the
secret concerning her new feelings for Paul, as her mother
enjoins her to (p.121). But this injunction comes after a scene in
which Virginie, to her immense relief, has been able to confess
those same new feelings to her mother. A new bond of trust has
been sealed between mother and daughter. Throughout the
confusion of motives and opinions which characterise the events
leading to her departure, Virginie behaves as the dutiful
daughter. Her one lapse from virtue (in her eyes, but hardly in
those of her mother or of the reader) is her admission to Paul of
her love, under the emotional pressure of their last passionate
conversation together (p.126). For the rest her acceptance of her
obligation to go to Europe is a mark of her constancy, or her
virtue understood in that sense. Above all, the constancy of her
virtue coincides with the constancy of her love: 'C'est pour toi
que je pars' (p.126). It is her vow to return to Paul which at last

calms his fury, that same fury which has just made him utter the fateful curse. Thus, at the high emotional point of her departure, love and virtue coincide: to leave Paul is a sacrifice which she makes for his sake. This is a third motive alongside her duty to respect her mother's wish and what she believes to be the will of God. Her vow is a response in the immediate context to Paul's passionate outburst (p.127), and it could in that sense be interpreted as a result of passion, of being carried away by an uncontrollable feeling. On the other hand, it does express her deepest aspiration and set on a new footing the promise that has always been there throughout their lives: the intention that they should marry, initially their mothers', thinking on their behalf, is now sealed as their own. The themes of passionate love and virtue are at this point become one, and they continue to be so for the rest of the book (cf. p.144).

This tendency to equate love and virtue is a characteristic of late eighteenth-century French ethical and aesthetic thought, and appears in Bernardin's *Etudes*: 'L'amour prend dans les âmes pures tous les caractères de la religion et de la vertu' (*4*, III, p.138). If we look at the context where the Old Man produces his much-quoted rousseauistic definition of virtue, we find that it is instantly interpreted by Paul as a reflexion about Virginie and not as an injunction to patience to himself. Paul finds the constancy and patience of virtue more difficult than Virginie. Certainly, the philosophic reading which the Old Man recommends (p.152) is no match for the image of the faithful Virginie. That image raises Paul's courage and inspires him to complete the repair of the valley garden after its devastation in the summer of her departure (p.153). The context tells us that love and virtue are equated, whatever the fine print of the Old Man's definition. This too is the key to our understanding of Virginie's fatal refusal to disrobe in order to save herself from the shipwreck. No amount of argument can make this extraordinary episode acceptable to modern tastes, but if virtue is present in her refusal, as the prosopopeia claims (p.170), we should see it as a symbolic act in terms of her love for Paul: her naked body is for his eyes only and her gesture is a part of the same constancy which has made her refuse an advantageous marriage at Court and the inheritance of her great-aunt's fortune. If, to us, such constancy appears as an unlikely competitor with the instinct for self-preservation (so much so that some commentators have endeavoured to equate Virginie's *pudeur* with European corruption!), then at least it is consistent with the close association of love and virtue throughout the second half of the tale. Looked at in this way, the gesture is something done specifically for her lover's sake and not merely for the sake of some general notion of womanhood. Bernardin has himself pointed us toward this interpretation in the description of the discovery of the drowned girl's body, still (most unrealistically) in the attitude which she has struck at the moment of perishing on the ship. *Pudeur* and love are both expressed by it: one hand holds her clothes, the other tightly grips Paul's portrait. The gesture of *pudeur* is a mark of constancy in love (p.160).

I have insisted elsewhere that for Bernardin, as for Rousseau before him, the naturalness of *pudeur* is a fact (see *16*). Not only is the point clear from the dénouement of *Paul et Virginie*, the idea itself is stated, and given a philosophical foundation, in the section of the twelfth *Etude* called 'Du sentiment de l'amour'. His view of this aspect of human nature is unequivocal: 'La nature a mis dans son cœur cet obstacle [de la pudeur], qui y triomphe souvent du plus doux des penchants et de la plus fougueuse des passions' (*4*, III, p.133). It remains only for him to explain the phenomenon as a struggle between, on the one hand, the *sens de l'amour*, the culmination of all physical sensation, and, on the other hand, the aspiration (or *sentiment*) towards the divine, both of which are strong in adolescents: 'La pudeur vient à mon avis du combat de ces deux puissances; et voilà pourquoi les enfants n'en ont point naturellement' (*4*, III, p.134).

There are clear aesthetic imperatives which require that Virginie should die, and her demise even has a mythical appeal (cf. *14*, p.59). The elegiac structure of the piece, apart from anything else, precludes any happy ending. The ideal quality of the feelings portrayed also rules out any thought that we should be allowed to see Paul and Virginie bringing up many children in the abject poverty feared by Mme de la Tour: once Virginie is disinherited by her great-aunt, the pair, now old enough to marry, face only that prospect of poverty. Death, we may say, is a function of idealisation. Nevertheless, even Virginie's symbolic dying gesture is comprehensible once we take the book's attitudes to *sentiment* and Nature into account. It is an affirmation of the absolute quality of their love: Virginie dies rather than compromise the standards which she believes her love requires her to uphold. The only conceivable home for such absolute feeling is the Elysium evoked in the prosopopeia (p.171).

In Virginie, then, love and virtue are identified and both serve an absolute, ideal, human nature. Paul, on the other hand, remains a creature of simple passion. From the very first, some readers have reacted to the philosophical dialogue of the second half in the manner of Mme Necker, regarding it as a 'bucketful of ice'. Here, it is true, the irritating didacticism is at its most overt. Paul's ingenuousness seems merely the excuse to draw forth the Old Man's sermons. It is, however, part of a consistent picture of the young man and of his reactions throughout the second half. First, he responds passionately to Virginie's departure, revisiting all her favourite island sites (pp.128-30). Then he asks to be made literate in order to communicate with her. Love made him a gardener, now it makes him a philosopher the moment his beloved goes away (pp.130-31). Love drives Paul's actions, sentiment is his motor, but not in the same manner as Virginie: his virtue is not brought to the fore. His feelings are an uncomplicated reaction to the inescapable situation which he finds himself in, while Virginie will be called upon to resist the temptations of fortune which Europe offers. Even his enjoyment of literature in the shape of *Télémaque* is purely in terms of his love for Virginie (p.131). The negative aspect of literature is that the licentious picture of European society presented in so many other novels increases his sense of privation and his fears of losing her (p.131). The extreme, passionate expression of this feeling (and to the modern eye a ridiculous one) is his response to the papaw-tree on the Old Man's homestead (pp.140 and 145): he alternately wishes to

chop it down in order to curtail the painful memories, and hugs
it as a talisman of Virginie. Such oscillations of feeling are
characteristic of the passions aroused by Paul's simple and
direct reflexions on his situation: the reason is intimately
associated, in Bernardin's scheme of things, with the passions of
corrupt society (cf. *9*, p.266).

The dialogue begins with Paul expressing his artless aspiration
to make a success in Europe for the sake of Virginie. The Old
Man counters this with descriptions of what Europe is 'really'
like. Paul, fearing for Virginie's integrity in such an environment, is reassured by the Old Man's repetition of the equation
between virtue and love (p.148). This leads on, via a further
series of innocent questions, to reflexions on European women,
marriage, attitudes to work and attitudes to leisure. The series
concludes with Paul eliciting the definition of virtue from the
Old Man (p.150). Even this does not still Paul's passions, as he
oscillates between the enthusiastic certainty that a virtuous
Virginie will return, and the despairing fear that he will lose her
for good. The Old Man's recommended cure for this passionate
state, namely philosophic literature, produces in Paul a response
which is almost amusing in its candour and directness: Virginie's
presence is a better solace than any philosophy (p.152)!

Paul's failure to show the courage of virtue in his reaction to
the final catastrophe is therefore thoroughly in character: only
his love made his deprivation bearable. When his beloved no
longer lives, there is nothing to sustain him: 'La douleur l'avait
submergé' (p.171). His weaker animal nature is victorious, and
he seeks repose in death rather than struggle to live on in his
grief. No doubt the series of deaths at the end appears contrived
and convenient. Yet even here an aesthetic 'logic' is in force: just
as the ideal quality of love and virtue is guaranteed by Virginie's
death, so too for the rest of the valley community there is no
future, other than in Elysium, once she is no longer with them
on Earth. The dénouement, indeed, is a confirmation,
negatively, of the equation of love and virtue: virtue's energy
ceases if death breaks the bond of love.

The idea of Heaven or Elysium is the ultimate guarantee of
the book's values, in particular the absoluteness of love and

virtue and their harmony with the laws of Nature. But it is an ambiguous Heaven: a reward and a fulfilment for Virginie, the prize for her virtue and constancy; but also a retreat and a refuge for the others, and indeed for the reader, who is offered the thought that the lost world of the natural, bemoaned by the elegy, actually lives on. If Heaven is a retreat and not the final goal of a struggle, an uneasy feeling about the morality of sensibility is bound to result. It is almost as if Elysium itself were being treated as a kind of Arcadia. Bernardin appears to fall into the trap, specifically indicated by Schiller, of compromising the ideal by indulging his own and the reader's emotional need. And the impression is not helped by the cross-current of conventional morality, in which, by contrast with the eternal felicity of the good, the great-aunt is punished (pp.173-74). We may say, however, despite these impressions, that he has at least tried to present the great-aunt's punishment as the consummation of her own misguided values: 'ce qui acheva la fin d'une si déplorable existence fut le sujet même auquel elle avait sacrifié les sentiments de la nature' (p.174). Her precious fortune goes to people she hates. Another uncomfortable point about the dénouement is that the Old Man's long final attempt to console Paul is also an almost explicit statement of why the tale must end as it does: there will be nothing ideal about the hero and heroine living on with many children in the kind of poverty that Virginie had earlier helped to alleviate.

5. Sensibility and Poetic Form

Discussion of sensibility thus far has been drawn towards the content of ideas. *Paul et Virginie*, however, is a *pastorale*, set in an elegiac frame and with an emphasis on the poetic possibilities of the genre. The book is not only 'about' innocent love in the tropics, it is also itself a kind of love-song. That is, sensibility has been written into the very form of the text, and our emotional responses depend as much on that form as they do on discursive statements about feeling and on explicit comparisons of feeling with Nature. The most appropriate analogy here is with music.

The 'musicality' of an author's prose, even when we are forced to recognise it, still today does not of itself command respect for him. Bernardin is neglected by critics despite a consensus about his considerable contribution to the revitalisation of the French literary language. That contribution is conceded to him (by implication as a relatively minor one) as critics express their reservations about his qualities as novelist, moralist or scientist. Furthermore his poetic prose, when critical attention is paid to it, tends to be analysed only in microcosm: his quest for balance and harmony in his sentences, his introduction of sound and colour into descriptions of Nature. Both of these points are of course valid, even important, and they would both apply equally well to a text such as the *Voyage*. But they say little about his claims to a broader and more impressive achievement.

Discussion of poetic prose requires some caution. The introduction of the musical analogy calls for still more. First of all, we may measure discourse, in general terms, according to a continuous scale which runs from the prosaic at one end to the highly poetic at the other. We call 'prosaic' that which signifies nothing apart from what the bare words 'stand for', a discourse which is something like a calculus. A report or a scientific article will be prosaic in this sense. We call 'poetic' a discourse which

PAUL ET VIRGINIE: SYNOPTIC SKETCH OF FORM

First half

a   81-82   The setting and narrators:
      81-82   Two cabins and landscape
      82   Authorial narrator meets Old Man

b   82-87   The valley settlement, its establishment and economy

c   87-92   'Microcosm' of the remainder of the first half:
      87-90   Rapid sketch of children's life: problem of their future
      90-92   Great-aunt and first letter. La Bourdonnais

      92-128   THE PRESENCE OF VIRGINIE

d   92-99   Rivière Noire adventure

e   99-113   The idyll:
      99-105   The place – details of the valley
      105   Elegiac reflexion
      105-11   Readings, picnics, drama, philanthropy
      111-12   Elegiac reflexion: a timeless Eden
      112-13   'Love duet'

f   113-24   The children's separation is prepared:
      113-17   Virginie's sexuality; torrid weather; a storm
      117-18   Children's future discussed: two solutions refused
      118-19   Great-aunt's new letter: summons to France; wealth
      119-21   La Bourdonnais visits the valley
      121-24   Virginie focus of attention and persuasion

g   124-28   Moonlight scene: last conversation of Paul and Virginie

Second half

      128-53   THE ABSENCE OF VIRGINIE

g   128-31   Paul's reactions:
      128-30   Wanderings and visitation
      130-31   Literacy and learning

b   131-36   Virginie's letter:
      131-34   The letter, enclosing Eu
      134-35   Paul's reply; European s
      135-36   False rumours of Virgin marriage in Europe

e   136-53   Philosophical interlude
      136-40   Old Man's solitude and character, with landsca
      140-53   Dialogue of Old Man a

f   153-62   Virginie's return:
      153-59   Arrival and shipwreck
      159-62   Funeral and apotheosis

d   163-71   Futile attempts to console Paul:
      163-66   Wanderings in unfamiliar place
      166-71   Old Man's 'monologue', inclu
      170-71   Prosopopeia of Virgin

c   171-74   Deaths:
      171-72   The mother's premonitory d
      173-74   All but the Old Man die

a   174-75   Elegiac epilogue and echo cf the oper

(Marginal brackets indicate the matching ternary structure in each half, and marginal letters a second 'set' of corresponding passages. Passages *a*, *e* and *g* also mark a certain structural symmetry.)

exploits, to some creative end, the further potentialities of language: its powers of analogy, of association, of evocation and so on. The poetic potential is an open-ended one: it is impossible to predict the new uses and combinations which may arise.

The 'prosaic' and the 'poetic' are the two terms of our scale, but the scale itself may be used to measure either prose or verse. The distinction between the prosaic and the poetic is in no way identical with a contrast between prose and verse. Prose may be highly poetic, as the nineteenth century has taught us, and verse may be prosaic, as some eighteenth-century examples would show. There is little need, therefore, for a lengthy defence of the idea of poetic prose. However, we may go on to divide poetic qualities themselves into two broad kinds: some are analogous to those of music and some are not. Broadly speaking, poetry is unlike music in so far as it depends on the denotation of concepts: the denotation of concepts is not entirely beyond the powers of music, but it is the exception rather than the rule. The denotative aspects of the poetic language of *Paul et Virginie* are, of course, the most conspicuous ones, and some of them we have seen already: descriptions of the exotic setting, models of evocation in their economy and clarity; the noble similes, also scrupulously clear, illustrating the human relationships; and the symbolic correspondences established between Nature and the workings of the human heart, as in the first cyclone (pp.115-16).

Features of poetry may resemble features of music in two ways: through rhythm (which may or may not subsume variations of tempo) and through the sonority of vowels and consonants, analogous to musical timbre. Musical pitch, on the other hand, has no linguistic counterpart. 'Timbre', through such obvious devices as assonance and alliteration or in more subtle ways, can, in poetic language, have a considerable power in underscoring the conceptual force of a text. I shall not pursue Bernardin's use of this, but rather concentrate on rhythm. There are two reasons for this emphasis, apart from the constraints of space. First, rhythm is the fundamental quality of music. Whereas patterns of repetition, variation and contrast in the pitch and timbre of musical sounds are not absolutely essential, such patterns in their duration (and by extension, tempo) are indispensable. Secondly, in Bernardin's poetic prose, rhythm, at the level of the sentence or at the level of the deployment of more extensive portions of text, is perhaps the most important, and certainly the most neglected, feature.

Because we are dealing in this chapter with an overall literary technique, or cluster of techniques, in which a precise connection between form and meaning cannot be pointed to, our quest is a delicate one, and fraught with the danger perhaps of manufacturing arguments where really there are none. But we do know what we are looking for: features which are expressive without being discursively explicit. Two detailed examples, as precise as they can be, will illustrate, at the outset, what is meant and help us to pick our way through the pitfalls. Both examples imply a reading of the text either literally aloud or 'inwardly' at the speed of speech. This is a point of crucial importance, since it has become habitual to read novels not so much 'with the ear' as 'with the eye', often at a pace far in excess of that of speech. Not only was reading aloud much more common in the social and literary world that Bernardin knew, he also quite specifically gave readings aloud of his novel in the salons, before its publication, as a kind of test or trial of its appeal. The prose of *Paul et Virginie* is addressed to our inward ear and deserves the attention which that implies. Now to our two illustrative examples.

Virginie begins to feel her 'mal', that is, to become sexually aware, and a correspondence is quickly established between this experience and the intolerably oppressive summer heat (pp.114-15). We thus have a characteristic example of an anthropomorphic Nature mirroring the moods of Man: the oppressiveness of the summer matches the oppressiveness of the new and disturbing 'heat' within. This correspondence is, of course, fixed discursively through the notions of heat, of wilting and wasting which Bernardin associates with both experiences. However he also, in some of the crucial sentences, renders this sense of oppressiveness non-discursively (and almost certainly unconsciously) by a repetition, three times, of one syllabic pattern. One may surely for this purpose, in prose, discount mute 'e's:

La terre se fendait de toutes parts;	l'herbe était brûlée;
des exhalaisons chaudes sortaient	du flanc des montagnes,
et la plupart de leurs ruisseaux	étaient desséchés.
Aucun nuage ne venait	du côté de la mer.

(p.114)

The repetition of the groups of eight syllables followed by five, almost as in verse, underlines, for the 'ear', that is, for the musical sense, the explicit effect of stifling monotony contained in the discourse. For good measure the fourth line is a prose alexandrine of twelve syllables. The rhythmic evenness within its two half-lines is in keeping with the stillness of the scene.

A more famous piece of poetic prose is the description of Virginie's midnight bathe during the same oppressive summer. One small example from this exceptionally rich passage must suffice. Again the obsessive presence of the girl's nascent sexuality is rendered by the device of repetition, not this time of a 'scansion' of the sense groups, but of a grammatical structure in which the pronoun subject 'elle' constantly recurs in the initial position alongside a historic present tense which, though strictly equivalent to a past historic, conveys a sense of intolerable duration and immediacy: 'Elle s'achemine', 'elle en aperçoit', 'Elle se plonge', 'Elle se rappelle' and 'Elle entrevoit' (pp.114-15). The reader's sensuality is appealed to through the imagery in the discursive sense of the words, but the most intimate sense of the girl's subjectivity is conveyed non-discursively by the rhythmic 'pulse'. The words speak of heat and cool, light and shade, flesh and water, present sensation and past memory, but the repetition of their form renders the feeling of oppression and obsession.

In both of these cases, therefore, we can clearly see the connection between human feeling and the formal, non-discursive means employed to express it. This, so to speak, is the microcosmic scale of the text's resemblance to music. Taking now the global scale of the work as a whole, it is easy enough to see the patterns of repetition, variation and contrast in the relationship between the different component sections of the text, but not so easy to put the finger on the feelings they evoke. One is reduced to vague assertions about Bernardin's 'oceanic' feeling for the oneness and balance of Nature. Yet unity and balance are the key terms: the unity of Man with Nature and the equilibrium of opposing forces within Nature: 'La nature a tout balancé' (p.150). This notion of the harmony of contrasting forces in Nature is one of the pet ideas of the *Etudes*. It is, therefore, not absolutely far-fetched to consider the fundamental binary structure of *Paul et Virginie* as a sort of formal and non-discursive exemplification of the idea and for that reason an effective rounding-off to the fourth volume of the *Etudes*.

Between, on the one hand, the exploitation of the non-discursive expressiveness of rhythm and form at the level of the sentence and, on the other hand, the presentation of an 'oceanic' feeling for Nature through the dynamic structure of the text as a whole, we find many features which achieve, on an intermediate scale, a comparable expressiveness via poetic form. The text's division into two halves is already intimately related to the rhythm of the feelings of the principal characters: the first half shows their innocent union with Nature and then the onset of passion, while the second pictures their separation from one another. The shape of the text itself conveys the sense of the inevitable changeability of things made explicit by the Old Man at the halfway point (p.128). The first half was the day, the second is the night. And yet, as if to remind us that it is the same world which turns, there are everywhere echoes, at the same time as variations, between the two halves. They echo each other, first of all, in their basic ternary structure: between two passages presenting almost exclusively facts and incidents, is framed a significant section, the main feature of which is to modify the reader's sense of time. These two central sections, which tend to attract adverse critical comment because nothing much happens in them, are in fact essential ones as far as sensibility is concerned. The first-half idyll (pp.99-113) establishes the harmony of innocent love with Nature, as both adolescents are present in the valley: while the second-half dialogue (pp.141-53) is a reflexion of Virginie's absence, in which time hangs heavy and

Paul attempts to come to terms with his pain.

In each of these central passages the non-discursive expressiveness of form contributes to the manipulation of time, and thereby, in each, to the dominant emotion. First, the Rivière Noire adventure is dissociated from the chronological sequence which has previously obtained; and secondly, the idyll starts (from p.100) with an effective flashback: 'Paul, à l'âge de douze ans'. The Rivière Noire adventure begins with a descriptive imperfect tense and the vague time reference 'un dimanche' (p.92). We infer that it is subsequent chronologically to the episode of the great-aunt's letter only from its position in the text. After that adventure, the text reverts (p.99) to a general descriptive imperfect to note the harmony and happiness of the two families. From this tense there is a shift into the pluperfect to note the attitudes that the women in particular had had to adopt in order to establish that harmony (p.100). And this pluperfect is the one in which the beginning of Paul's landscaping is described. In turn the narrative set in train by these two tenses is used in itself as a miniature frame for past historics to describe the Old Man's inscriptions (pp.102-03). It is impossible to link these past historics to a date, and they even in the end become interchangeable with an imperfect: 'Mais Virginie n'approuvait pas mon latin. "J'eusse mieux aimé", ajoutait-elle, "TOUJOURS AGITÉE, MAIS CONSTANTE." — "Cette devise", lui répondis-je, "conviendrait encore mieux à la vertu."' (p.103).

Bernardin brings us back, through the description of the Repos de Virginie, approximately to the time of the great-aunt's first letter, but only obliquely, thanks to references to the growth together of the two coconut trees after twelve years (p.104). This, however, is cunningly combined with a flashback to the time of the trees' planting: thus the episode which brings us back 'up to date' is also the one which returns us the furthest into the past! The rest of the idyll is presented in imperfect tenses as if the activities were habitual: the different routines of summer and winter, the readings, the picnics, the philanthropy. Yet this too is a piece of time-manipulation, since, if we are to think of all these activities as being engaged in by the adolescents (that is, not by the children when younger), then they can have done them at most for only one summer and winter. The various uses of tense thus combine to give the semblance of permanence to the adolescents' life in the valley. They tend, by their accumulation as much as by their meaning, to expand the fleeting instant into a whole existence at one with Nature: time is, as it were, 'cancelled' by these procedures — time, separate from the rhythms of Nature, is not part of their experience (p.111). Bernardin is astute enough to keep back this explicit reference to time until almost the end of the idyll. A sense of the youngsters' own experience is rendered non-discursively through the 'narrative pace' of the text.

The manipulation of time is assisted, in the first half only, by another device. The story is told twice, or almost: first rapidly and then in a more extended, or 'slower' form. A binary principle is visibly operative on both occasions. A rapid sequence of two contrasted passages, the sketch of childhood (pp.87-90) and the section concerning the great-aunt and her first letter (pp.90-92), introduces all the first half's essential themes and problems. This sequence is echoed, much expanded, by the Rivière Noire adventure plus idyll on the one hand, and the events leading to Virginie's departure (pp.113-24) on the other. The shorter pair of passages and the longer stand in relationship to each other rather as an overture does to an opera: we hear all the significant themes, but we do not yet know how things will work out. Our subconscious recognition of the rhythmic resemblance between the two sequences combines with the fact that, for the most part, the shorter sequence and the longer cover the same ground chronologically, to give the impression of time standing still. The rhythm and the narrative pace of the text are a non-discursive representation of the pre-vailing mood.

The philosophical dialogue (pp.140-53), which in the second half corresponds to the idyll in the first, is also vital to the dimension of time, but now, by contrast, conveys the sharp and painful consciousness of that dimension. No longer at one with himself, his family and Nature, Paul's thoughts are always with Virginie, that is, elsewhere but in the here and now. Time is not so much 'cancelled' or suspended, as it was in the idyll, it is rather 'hanging heavy'. Little happens apart from description and talk: the only truly significant fact at this period is the absence of the heroine; it is waiting time. The passage of time is alluded to intermittently and in different ways in this section: by reference to a tree planted by Virginie (p.140), or by Paul's wish-fulfilling thoughts that she is about to come home (p.151). This last reference, incidentally, can easily be misread: 'Virginie n'avait point écrit, parce qu'elle allait arriver'. In its context this is not a piece of telling by the Old Man, but a description of Paul's thoughts, or habitual utterances, in *style indirect libre*: we are reading that special kind of indirect speech which translates the exact words or thoughts of the reported speaker into the pre-vailing tense of the reporting narrative. Also, however boring the modern reader finds the philosophising, the section does have an element of plot: things European, and how they are to be viewed, do have interest for Paul, since that is where Virginie is, and where his mind is focussed. He becomes literate, is curious, and starts to read, because he has moved from inno-cence into experience and from a timeless existence into one of self-consciousness and pain. This, indeed, is his only need of philosophy. His state of soul is shown by his need of European culture. By its length and position, therefore, the philosophical interlude, consisting for the most part of the dialogue, has an expressive function independent of its discursive content: the form makes time hang heavy for us as it hangs heavy for Paul.

The Rivière Noire adventure and the Old Man's defence of solitude and description of his homestead are part of the middle phase in each ternary structure (pp.92-99 and 136-40), since both contribute to the manipulation of time. However, these two sections, taken individually, are a pendant to each other in another way: uncultivated nature is the backcloth to both. In one the children are together in the wilderness, and in the second the solitude of separation is expressed in terms of it. In the one the children move through wild nature almost as part of it, bene-fiting from its fruits, and swallowed up by it when it threatens. Only in the second half is there occasion for picturesque description, the product of melancholy contemplation of the wild. A common feature of these two passages, apart from the

identical natural backcloth, is that both take us away from the
little valley: herein is the quality of echo. However, whereas in
the Rivière Noire adventure the valley is still a focus, the point of
departure and of return, the solitude of the Old Man's
homestead involves a complete displacement. Indeed, everything
that is significant in the second half, or most of it, happens away
from home. Just as Virginie is absent from the island, so we the
readers are displaced from the centre of the idyll of the first half.
The text thus gains in symbolism and avoids the pitfall of
repetition. The binary structure of form contributes in yet
another way to the basic sentimental motif of presence and
absence. One piece in the jig-saw of elegy is in its place.

Other structural correspondences between the two halves run,
as it were, in counterpoint to the ternary structure. First, there is
a degree of symmetry to the text if we take the division between
the two halves as the centre line. The most obvious case is the
short pages at the beginning and at the end: both are an image of
the desolate solitude of the high valley. They differ only in that
the final pages are much more emotionally charged. They are
like the powerful codas of some symphonies, where an opening
motif has returned at the end, but emotionally transformed by
what has been heard in between. The symmetry in the two
developments either side of the centre line is not quite so obvious
(pp.124-28 and 128-31). There is a close emotional connection
between them to the extent that Paul, who in his final interview
with Virginie has evoked the sophisticated life that she will lead
in France, reacts ultimately by attempting to emulate her in the
quest for literacy and learning. There is also the still more
evident point that his re-visitation of the sites beloved of Virginie
is a direct expression of the violent emotion found also in the
interview. Finally, and slightly more tenuously, the idyll and the
philosophical interlude (pp.99-113 and 135-53) find themselves
in corresponding, symmetrical positions, if we follow the seven
sub-sections of each half away from the centre line.

The two 'pivotal' passages, on either side of the division
between the two halves, are paired together in another counter-
pointing set of correspondences parallel with the ternary
structure. This time the 'set', comprising seven sub-sections in

each half, has no shape of its own, but it does, significantly, pair together the idyll and philosophical interlude yet again. These passages thus find themselves in a position of strong rhythmic emphasis, a position of key importance to the expression of feeling and mood. Two other significant balancing passages of the new 'set' are in equivalent positions in respect of the ternary structure, and both have a tragic strain: the narrative of events leading to Virginie's departure in the first half (pp.113-24) and the equally eventful account of the shipwreck, funeral and apotheosis of Virginie in the second (pp.153-62). In this set of correspondences, however, the Rivière Noire adventure pairs not with the Old Man's solitude and homestead, but with the Old Man's futile attempts to console Paul after Virginie's death (pp.163-71). The Old Man and Paul have even gone off in a similar geographical direction, towards the Plaines Williams. The earlier adventure takes the form of a short journey followed by a longer account of the children becoming lost. The later passage also starts with a short, and equally futile, excursion, and Paul, in the ensuing speech by the Old Man, is now a lost soul in a deeper and much more serious sense. Virginie speaks with moral authority in both cases, though admittedly much more briefly in the earlier episode.

The affinities, in this 'set', between the remaining passages from each half are perhaps less striking, but no less real. Thus the rapid relation of the deaths of all but Virginie (pp.173-74) corresponds clearly to the equally rapid sketch of the children's early life (pp.87-90), since life and death are an obvious balancing contrast. In a different way, Virginie's letter of the second half (pp.131-34) is a pendant to the expositional passage recounting the mothers' settlement in the valley (pp.82-87). There has to be some account, or exposition, of Virginie's reception in France by her great-aunt, and the letter gives it. The opening and closing pages I have already mentioned, and there remains only the scene of the moonlight goodbyes in the first half (pp.124-28) and the account of Paul's first reactions to Virginie's leaving (pp.128-31), which we have already seen to be in symmetry on either side of the centre line.

Now, it is hard to say to what extent Bernardin strove consciously for these correspondences of form. We do know, on the other hand, that they are finally achieved, as is the overriding binary structure itself, only in the very last stages of the creative process, after the manuscript draft of the *Histoire de Mlle Virginie de la Tour* (see 2). It is remarkable that we are able to 'pair' specific passages from each half and to find that they correspond with each other in length, thematic material, and sometimes internal rhythm, to the extent that they do. Like the patterns of repetition, variation and contrast in a musical composition, these correspondences are vital to the coherence and interest of the whole piece. They perform, in that sense, some of the usual functions of story and plot. We are held not so much by a crude desire to know what happens next, nor by the curiosity to know why it happens, since, apart from the confusion of motives surrounding Virginie's departure for France, the answers are self-evident; we are held rather by the underlying binary rhythm of feeling in the book, and the satisfaction of subconsciously recognising the correspondences between the two halves. The aesthetic satisfaction offered through the repetitions and variations in the form reinforces the emotions aroused by the basic elegiac contrast.

Above all, the text's correspondences of form help to establish a feeling of inexorable necessity in the narrative. As in good music, we feel that it could not proceed to its end in any manner but the one it follows. The structure emphasises what we know from the beginning: the huts must end in ruin. Our dearest wish throughout is that they should not, and this is the strongest twist which is given to the elegiac emotion: the tension between our wishes for the hero and heroine and what we know must come to pass. The sense of necessity is, of course, discursively explicit as well as expressed through the form, principally thanks to the Old Man's lamenting references to the desolate present. Bernardin makes the impression still more unmistakable by a simple system of premonitions. In Fabre's words: 'La mort est présente d'un bout à l'autre de *Paul et Virginie*, pastorale promise à la tragédie, et un naïf mais nécessaire système de prémonitions n'en laisse rien ignorer' (7, p.172). From the very opening panorama of the island, details selected for mention are the Baie du Tombeau and Cap Malheureux, names which Bernardin will later attribute, quite fictitiously, to the *Saint-Géran* disaster. For the erudite reader, or at least the reader armed with a footnote, there is a premonition in the comparison of Paul and Virginie to the children of Niobe, slaughtered by a jealous rival of their mother (*1*, p.92 and note 1). Furthermore, some of the tales read to the children on winter nights concern shipwrecks on desert islands (p.106). Still more significantly premonitory is young Paul's daring game of swimming out to the reefs and, by a rapid return, dodging the enormous ocean breakers. Virginie screams with fearful concern for him (p.108). Other examples can no doubt be found.

The most important aspects of the text's non-discursive expressiveness, and the most difficult to do justice to, are these structural ones, since they help us to establish alternative genre criteria to those often stressed when assessing fiction. They show that instead of rich and complex story, plot and characters, we are to look for rich nuances and variations of human feeling, evoked not only in the denotative sense of the text, but also in its rhythms and form. These aspects are what give the tale its organic unity. The text is 'organic' rather than episodic in the sense that no one part of it could be removed without serious damage to the whole. The parts make sense only in terms of the whole. To that extent, *Paul et Virginie* is more like the classic fiction of the nineteenth century than it is like many earlier novels, even a good one such as Marivaux's *Le Paysan parvenu*, from which the various scenes can easily be detached and enjoyed quite separately from the rest. The difference, in the case of Bernardin's novel, is that the organic unity is achieved poetically, more through the subtleties of form than through a complex organisation of ideas and human relationships. A few further details will help to emphasise its richness.

Concerning the dialogue, Vivienne Mylne rightly stresses its affinity with the *style noble* of verse tragedy (*10*, p.250). Unlike tragedy, however, and more in common with the prose of *drame bourgeois*, it must perforce contain references to everyday objects. Bernardin's dialogue is, at any rate, consistent with a certain poetic stylisation and formalisation of tone, which has a

similar motive to that in French classical tragedy: it removes
distractions from the principal centre of interest, namely human
passion and feeling. Stylisation and elevation of tone help us to
concentrate on the universal human qualities of sensibility. This
characteristic is also entirely in keeping with the idealisation
which elegy always involves. Within this general, but essential,
observation, we may identify three uses of dialogue in *Paul et
Virginie*: dialogue as argument, or philosophical dialogue, as in
the second half between Paul and the Old Man; dialogue in its
familiar role of conversation; and dialogue as 'aria'. The latter
concerns us particularly in this chapter, and I shall concentrate
on direct rather than indirect dialogue.

At two peaks of emotional intensity in the first half, we find
direct speech which does not so much convey information or
argument as represent an enthusiastic outpouring of feeling,
akin to the function of the operatic aria. The first of these cases
is the 'duo' which concludes the idyll (pp.112-13). Its introduction is, incidentally, an inept piece of technique undermining
the Old Man's narrative 'privilege': 'Quelquefois seul avec elle
(il me l'a mille fois raconté), il lui disait au retour de ses travaux:
"Lorsque je suis fatigué ta vue me délasse"' etc. We should not
even wonder how he might know this information if he did not
tell us. However, the direct speech which follows, like the
biblical Song of Solomon, is a hymn of praise by Paul to his
beloved. It contains only one emotion, repeatedly expressed in
many variations, namely awe at how he can feel so much love
for his 'sister'. The opening assertions are followed by
wondering questions: 'Dis-moi par quel charme tu as pu
m'enchanter' (p.112), but the message of love is the same
throughout, and recurs in his final offer of a comb of honey and
his invitation to her to come to his arms. The progression of this
passage is that of a song. There is absolutely no need for little
snatches of doggerel *à la* Florian when we have lyricism like this.
However, the language of the 'song' is, in Schiller's terms,
'sentimental': that is, it is not what an ingenuous, natural
adolescent in Paul's position would say, it is our idea, or ideal,
of what he might say. Our last quotation reflects the language of
the salons, as does: 'Lorsque je t'approche, *tu ravis tous mes*

sens' (p.112, my italics). This is perhaps the price we pay for our proximity to the *style noble*. Interestingly, in the complete early draft of this passage, Paul's language is much less sophisticated, partly perhaps because it was there attributed to an earlier moment of adolescence: 'je reviens près de toi avec tant de plaisir' (*2*, p.201). 'Sentimental' language may certainly be found in the early draft, but it becomes more developed in the later versions.

The impression of an 'aria' in this direct speech of Paul is emphasised when Virginie answers with a piece of similar length. There is also the habitual imperfect tense used to introduce both passages: 'Quelquefois seul avec elle... il lui disait', and 'Virginie lui répondait'. Like songs, their hymns of praise to each other are repeatable and repeated. As in an operatic duet, Virginie's speech answers both in kind (she praises him as he has praised her, in terms of the pleasure which the sight of him gives her) and literally to his wondering questions about her: people brought up together must love each other. This 'duo' rounds off the idyll, representing the culmination of the growth of their innocent love. In terms of the overall shape of the first half, however, and in terms of the progression of feeling, this 'duo' does not stand alone. Another one, more passionate and less innocently calm, corresponds to it at the end of the first half, in the final interview between the two. This time it occurs within something more recognisable as conversation (pp.125-27). We have the same simplicity of feeling as in the earlier case, the lover's accusation of cruelty for being willing to leave, Virginie's insistence that she leaves for his sake only and loves him still. This is a moment of high passion (p.126), since it shows Virginie succumbing, under the pressure of emotional pain, to her desire, despite her mother's injunction, to tell Paul her love. The resemblance in treatment between this and the earlier 'duo' calls to mind the differences in feeling between the two cases.

The high passion develops still more in two further 'arias' immediately afterwards, in which Paul's anger mounts to the point of pronouncing his 'curse' (may the sea never bring Virginie back), and is only quietened by her vow of faithfulness (p.127). From these passionate voices we move to the other, discursive, poetic mode in a fine simile: 'Comme le soleil fond et précipite un rocher de glace du sommet des Apennins, ainsi tomba la colère impétueuse de ce jeune homme à la voix de l'objet aimé' (p.127). Silence descends after the loud music of anger, and hero and heroine will never exchange words again. Another use of a kind of direct speech at a high emotional point is the prosopopeia of Virginie, pronounced by the Old Man in a last desperate attempt to console Paul (pp.170-71). This too is a love-song, from Elysium.

The two cyclones create another kind of formal correspondence between the two halves of the text. There is a clear symbolism in the first storm, quite independent of this correspondence. It is likened, by juxtaposition, to the natural, but disruptive, advent of sexuality. It is also, however, a kind of premonition of the later hurricane which destroys not only Virginie's innocence but also her life. Bernardin contrives, nevertheless, not to repeat himself in the two descriptions, since one is a landscape and the other a seascape. There is both repetition and variation, variation especially in the fact that the second cyclone lacks the symbolism of the first. Yet it receives more extended treatment because more hangs on it dramatically.

I have concentrated in this chapter on some of the 'strategic' aspects of the text's expressiveness through form, believing that their importance has been neglected by other critics, and believing also that any attentive reader, in the spirit of my two brief examples at the beginning, is capable of appreciating and analysing, on the microcosmic scale, the harmony of Bernardin's sentences and his unique ability in matching sound to sense. Taking these two aspects together, we have, I believe, his principal claim to literary greatness. They combine to create an organic novel, the poetic prose of which will bear comparison with better-known, later attempts to exploit, in fiction, the analogy between music and literature.

Conclusion

From the last chapter it will have become clear why I play down the undeniable 'satirical' strain in *Paul et Virginie*. I believe it to be a weakness, a deviation from the fundamentally elegiac stance of the author: it displaces us needlessly from the world of the ideal into an imperfect actuality and only makes us aware of the feebleness of Bernardin's ideas as suggested solutions. It is also a temptation to student and critic alike, since it is easier, by and large, to talk about social criticism than about sensibility and prose-poetic quality. I make no apology, therefore, for not elaborating on this blemish other than to say that it is there. Bernardin is too much a creature of his age, and too much a preacher himself, for his tendency to sermonise not to lead him down the 'satirical', or socio-critical path.

The last chapter also in my view provides the key to an issue which would deserve another book: the relationship of Bernardin to posterity, and in particular to Romanticism. In the Romantic age, music gradually becomes more important as compared with visual art, not only in its own right, but also as an aesthetic paradigm of literature; literature is no longer merely to 'represent' or 'reflect' reality, it is to create whole new worlds of the spirit and of imagination, in order to illuminate the real and the ordinary (see *19*). Bernardin, by his creative 'instinct' alone and with no campaigning theory of literary criticism to guide him, achieves, in this little masterpiece, a vibrant 'musicality': his novel 'sings' melodiously of a world more beautiful than the real, within our reach if only we had the faith and the spirit.

It is easy for the critic to miss this quality, to see Bernardin as merely the inventor, in his descriptions, of the literary picturesque, to take his portrayal of feeling as the last twitch of Ancien Régime sensibility, and to observe (perhaps tendentiously withal) that the *pastorale* ends with him. The more recent reputation of the work, admittedly, has not helped. Already by the middle of the nineteenth century it was considered chiefly as a book for children, and from there it is but a short step to thinking it childish, as Trahard's remarks on his own generation testify (*1*, p.i). Yet Bernardin's positive quality is real: the generations closer to him caught his song more readily than we do, and better appreciated the work's powerful mythical appeal. That appeal is reflected not so much in the number of editions produced until well into the nineteenth century, as in the quite remarkable iconography which grew up with them (see *18*). The early nineteenth century was, it is true, an age of innovation and development in ever cheaper techniques of book-illustration. *Paul et Virginie*, however, inspired visual representations not only in editions of the text, but also in painting, in cheap earthenware and expensive porcelain, and in the almost strip-cartoon style of popular *imagerie* such as the *images d'Epinal*, an especially inexpensive form of illustration available even from itinerant pedlars (compare the cover of our edition). It is almost as if some of these images functioned as secular icons, permanent windows through which to view the visionary world which Bernardin creates. There was even wallpaper depicting scenes from the book![3] The mythical appeal of the text is fourfold: the myth of the tropical paradise, given new life by his powers of evocation; the myth of innocent childhood, given memorable form through a relationship, whereas Rousseau's *Emile* had presented it more philosophically and in the abstract; the myth of a love which is 'meant to be' from the earliest moment of life, lent added force by its association with the idea of the family (much could doubtless be made of the fact that the families are fatherless); and finally the myth of death, death as the seal of purity.

There is even something in this novel of 'prophecy': not the foretelling of the future (although ecologists might be interested in the misgivings about the colonial economy), and not merely the preaching of righteousness, but a 'song' or musical strain which taps a deep well-spring of universal human emotion — in

[3] Entwistle, E.A., *French Scenic Wallpapers 1800-60* (Leigh-on-Sea, F. Lewis, 1972), p.37.

this case, the desire to feel ourselves part of the earth on which we tread (*21*, p.162). If Bernardin, on account of his *Etudes* and of *Paul et Virginie*, enjoyed enormous prestige and respect among his contemporaries, a standing which allowed him to survive the Revolution without selling his soul, it was perhaps because of this prophetic note in his work, a note picked out in Mme de Boisguilbert's description of him, in a letter of 27 August 1788 (just after the novel's publication), as a 'prophète dans son pays' (*6*, p.82). In order to recognise 'prophecy' in those select authors who have it, we must exercise humility and put our sense of humour into cold store. I am content if what I have written encourages my readers to do so.

Select Bibliography

Though select, the following list represents a sizeable proportion of the available critical material.

WORKS BY BERNARDIN DE SAINT-PIERRE

1. *Paul et Virginie*, texte établi, avec une introduction, des notes et des variantes, par Pierre Trahard (Paris, Garnier, 1958). Introduction rather diffuse; discussion of manuscripts superseded by no.2; valuable notes, variants and bibliography.
2. Veyrenc, Marie-Thérèse, *Edition critique du manuscrit de Paul et Virginie de Bernardin de Saint-Pierre intitulé: "Histoire de Melle Virginie de la Tour"* (Paris, Nizet, 1975). Detailed analysis of three manuscript states of the text (*ca* 1771-85) in parallel with the first edition of 1788.
3. *Voyage à l'Ile de France*, introduction et notes d'Yves Bénot (Paris, La Découverte, 1983).
4. *Etudes de la nature*, 3 vols (Paris, Didot, 1784).

BIOGRAPHY

5. Maury, F., *Etude sur la vie et les œuvres de Bernardin de Saint-Pierre* (Paris, Hachette, 1892). Turgid. Still of value on Bernardin's philosophy and aesthetics.
6. Souriau, M., *Bernardin de Saint-Pierre d'après ses manuscrits* (Paris, Société Française d'Imprimerie et de Librairie, Ancienne Librairie Lecène, Oudin et Cie, 1905). Sympathetic, readable, economical, historically sound.

CRITICAL STUDIES

7. Fabre, J., 'Une question de terminologie littéraire: *Paul et Virginie*, pastorale', *Etudes de littérature moderne*, II (1953), Faculté des Lettres de Toulouse. Also in his *Lumières et romantisme* (Paris, Klincksieck, 1963), pp.167-99 (references are to this version). Outstanding seminal study, still hardly heeded by successors.
8. Trahard, P., *Les Maîtres de la sensibilité française au XVIIIe siècle (1715-1789)*, IV (Paris, Boivin, 1932), pp.71-146. Important discussion. Treat with caution concerning Rousseau, the *conte moral* and evaluation of *Paul et Virginie*.

9. Mauzi, R., *L'Idée du bonheur dans la littérature et la pensée françaises au XVIIIe siècle* (Paris, Colin, 1965). Essential for situating Bernardin in the history of ethical ideas.

10. Mylne, Vivienne, *The Eighteenth-Century French Novel, Techniques of Illusion*, second edition (Cambridge University Press, 1981), pp.245-62. A sober, and representative, assessment of Bernardin's place in the historical development of narrative technique.

The recent periodical literature in English, including my own article, is striking in its emphasis on themes and ideas, and for the most part ignores Fabre's invitation to consider the text's 'poetry'.

11. Lowrie, Joyce O., 'The structural significance of sensual imagery in *Paul et Virginie*', *Romance Notes*, XII (1970-71), 351-56.

12. Cherpack, C., '*Paul et Virginie* and the myths of death', *Publications of the Modern Language Association of America*, XC (1975), 247-55. Important subject, self-indulgent discussion. Wrong on the dénouement.

13. Kisliuk, Ingrid, 'Le symbolisme du jardin et l'imagination créatrice chez Rousseau, Bernardin de Saint-Pierre et Chateaubriand', *Studies on Voltaire and the Eighteenth Century*, CLXXXV (1980). Also wrong on the dénouement.

14. Francis, R.A., 'Bernardin de Saint-Pierre's *Paul et Virginie* and the failure of the ideal state in the eighteenth-century French novel', *Nottingham French Studies*, XIII (1974), 51-60. Studies the adverse effects of Bernardin's didacticism. Useful ideas on Arcadia versus Utopia.

15. Runte, Roseann, '*La Chaumière indienne:* counterpart and complement to *Paul et Virginie*', *Modern Language Review*, LXXV (1980), 774-80. Follows up Bernardin's satire of contemporary science and academies.

16. Robinson, P., 'Virginie's fatal modesty: thoughts on Bernardin de Saint-Pierre and Rousseau', *British Journal for Eighteenth-Century Studies*, V (1982), 35-48. Historical discussion of the dénouement, contesting nos 12 and 13.

HISTORICAL, ICONOGRAPHICAL

17. D'Alméras, H., *'Paul et Virginie' de Bernardin de Saint-Pierre, histoire d'un roman* (Paris, Société Française d'Editions Littéraires et Techniques, 1937). Account of the real-life background of the novel, with documents.

18. Toinet, P., *'Paul et Virginie', répertoire bibliographique et iconographique* (Paris, Maisonneuve et Larose, 1963). Starting point for research.

19. Abrams, M.H., *The Mirror and the Lamp* (Oxford University Press, 1963). Studies the shifting of aesthetic paradigms from Classical to Romantic literature, with a notable emphasis on the increasing importance of the musical model.

20. Filliot, J.-M., *La Traite des esclaves vers les Mascareignes au XVIIIe siècle* (Paris, O.R.S.T.O.M., 1974). Pure economic and maritime history. Offers useful facts and perspectives on Mauritius.

THEORY OF THE NOVEL

21. Forster, E.M., *Aspects of the Novel* (London, Arnold, 1927). Seminal study of basic concepts, but unnecessarily derogatory about literary history.
22. Booth, Wayne, C., *The Rhetoric of Fiction* (University of Chicago Press, 1961). Brilliant analysis of most of the critical issues. Essential.

CRITICAL GUIDES TO FRENCH TEXTS

edited by

Roger Little, Wolfgang van Emden, David Williams